A RECIPE *for* PEACE

7 Ingredients for a *Satisfying Life*

Brenda Buckner

A RECIPE *for* PEACE

7 Ingredients for a
Satisfying Life

JANIE CRAUN

EDITOR OF *CHRISTIAN WOMAN*

Gospel Advocate Company
Nashville, Tennessee

Published by Gospel Advocate Co.
1006 Elm Hill Pike, Nashville, TN 37210
www.gospeladvocate.com

ISBN 10: 0-89225-577-3
ISBN 13: 978-0-89225-577-1

You will keep him in perfect peace,
Whose mind is stayed on You.

(Isaiah 26:3)

To my husband, Karl,
my friend and companion
for more than 40 years.

TABLE of CONTENTS

PREFACE

I would imagine that women have been collecting recipes for as long as there have been cooks. Our favorite dishes tend to become associated with the good friends who first prepared them and shared the results with us. Many of us have binders or boxes filled with cards and scraps of paper on which we have saved the carefully recorded directions for someone's specialty – like my Aunt Mary's Jam Cake or my mother-in-law's boiled custard.

Like me, you may collect cookbooks. And now that the Internet also provides access to recipes of all kinds, we have the tools needed to become successful cooks. What we often lack is the practice.

Many years ago I discovered a recipe for homemade yeast rolls that has become a favorite in our family. It appeared in a local newspaper, but since then I have seen similar recipes for Butterhorn Rolls in other publications. This one calls for seven basic ingredients that are common to most bread recipes: milk, shortening and eggs combined with sugar, yeast, salt and flour. Couple these ingredients with a careful adherence to the instructions, and the result is a homemade roll that is perfection itself!

It occurs to me that the teachings in the Bible are similar in some ways to the recipes we consult over and over again because we know they work. The Bible's 66 books make up a collection of spiritual recipes that are proven to be reliable. We are assured that when we put these instructions into practice, using the particular ingredients called for (no substitutions!), the result is going to be heavenly – a peace that "surpasses all understanding" (Philippians 4:7). So put on your aprons, and join me as we explore God's recipe for perfect peace. Once you've tasted it, I hope you'll be eager to share this one with others.

– Janie Craun

THE SEARCH FOR PEACE

The desire for peace must be as old as man himself. After Adam and Eve were driven from their home, life became extremely difficult. The Garden of Eden became a distant memory – a haven of serenity almost forgotten. Within a few generations, the earth was so filled with violence that God chose to destroy what He had created, preserving one man with his household (Genesis 6:13, 17-18). From then on, being able to live out one's life in peace would be considered a great blessing (15:15).

Since the earliest times, people of Hebrew descent have greeted each other with the word "shalom." Loosely translated, it means "Go in peace, and may you prosper." The thought, to this day, serves as a benediction among people of goodwill.

Aaron, the Lord's high priest, blessed those who came to worship God with the beautiful prayer found in Numbers 6:24-26: "The Lord bless you and keep you; The Lord make His face shine upon you, And be gracious to you; The Lord lift up His countenance upon you, And give you peace."

This is our prayer for all who begin this study today: "May the Lord give you peace."

CHAPTER 1

PEACE ON EARTH

I was born in 1945, just months before the end of World War II. Many of my family members had served the country in some way during the war effort. Several uncles were in the army, my dad and other relatives worked at the DuPont Co. making war materials, and my mom and an aunt worked briefly in Washington, D.C., as legal stenographers for the government.

The end of that conflict was cause for tremendous celebration. American servicemen came home, and a flood of baby boomers was born the following year. Expectations were high that ours would be a generation blessed with peace.

The Fabulous '50s

The decade of the 1950s followed, sometimes referred to as the Nifty Fifties or the Fabulous Fifties. The country was riding a wave of patriotism, and people were proud to be Americans. Many families enjoyed a degree of prosperity that allowed them to afford luxuries such as cars and televisions for the first time. Folks were going to church in record numbers, and most women were still stay-at-home moms.

But life was not as ideal as some remember. In 1952 the worst outbreak of polio in the nation's history claimed thousands of lives, many of them children. And once again U.S. citizens were being deployed – this time to Korea. An escalating Cold War with Russia created the threat of a nuclear attack and the spread of godless communism to America. This fear prompted Congress to amend our Pledge of Allegiance to say that we were "one nation *under God*."

The Turbulent '60s

By 1960 a new crisis had arisen – this time in Cuba. My generation had never experienced war on our continent, and it was a frightening possibility. The crisis ended under the leadership of our 35th president, John F. Kennedy, and the country celebrated again. We had dodged another bullet and hope was running high.

All that changed in November 1963 when President Kennedy was killed by a gunman as he rode through the streets of Dallas. The nation went into shock.

A new president took office, and another problem surfaced. This one was the practice of segregation, especially prevalent in the Deep South where it had existed since the Civil War. Inequities that needed to be corrected brought about the Civil Rights Movement in America. Legislation ultimately resulted in changes for the better, but they didn't come about peacefully. The movement's leader, Martin Luther King Jr., was assassinated in April 1968.

The Psychedelic '70s

By the 1970s the public was weary of war and conflict, and the "peace" emblem became symbolic of Americans' frustration. The country's involvement in Vietnam was especially unpopular. By the time U.S. servicemen had finally returned home, we were a nation divided and disillusioned. The catch phrase of a new generation became "make love, not war." The result was a "sexual revolution" in America, due in part to the development of the birth control pill (1960), legalized abortion (1973) and no-fault divorce that gradually spread throughout the country. The nation saw a significant increase in the number of broken homes and growing social problems in our society. Many of the biblical principles that had guided our nation in the past were openly challenged. And with the publication of Joseph Fletcher's *Situation Ethics* (1966), some were echoing Nietzche's sentiment that "God is dead."[1]

Fast forward 50 years, and our world has seen many changes – both good and bad. Industrialization has come to many backward nations, and modern technology is reshaping the way people live and think. To date, Christianity – despite the predictions of naysayers – has spread into almost every country in the world. But conflicts continue around the globe, with the threat of another world war always present.

At home other problems persist. Unemployment, inflation and deficit-spending pose economic challenges that will affect generations to come. Now a senior citizen, I can see the truth of Solomon's observation so long ago: "That which has been is what will be, That which is done is what will be done, And there is nothing new under the sun" (Ecclesiastes 1:9).

Lyrics from one popular song of the 1950s keep coming to mind: "Let there be peace on earth, and let it begin with me. Let there be peace on earth, the peace that was meant to be."[2] Decades later, the words are still relevant.

But Solomon was right. Wars and disease will continue, and sin will always be present. Our Lord knew that. Yet He left the beauty of heaven and entered into this troubled world to become the Prince of Peace.

Peace, Perfect Peace – Is It Possible?

Every generation has known its share of hard times. The Old Testament scriptures record periods of famine, pestilence and horrendous brutality. Faithful prophets of God were often tortured and silenced for speaking the truth. And basic morality, even among God's chosen people, was always fluctuating.

Against this backdrop of unrest and depression, the prophet Isaiah foresaw a time of "perfect peace." He wrote about a day when men whose minds were stayed on God would sing about it (Isaiah 26:3). Eventually, the prophet was put to death for his outspoken views. But he understood that true peace can live within the heart of a person even when things in the world are at their worst.

Before his death, Isaiah was given a glimpse of the One who would usher in that promised peace. He wrote:

> For unto us a Child is born, Unto us a Son is given; and the government will be upon His shoulder. And His name will be called Wonderful, Counselor, Mighty God, Everlasting Father, Prince of Peace (Isaiah 9:6).

Isaiah's vision was realized some 700 years later – on a night when the angels of heaven proclaimed "on earth peace, goodwill toward men" (Luke 2:14). That was the night when the Christ was born. But even that wonderful event was accompanied with unbelievable sorrow. News of His birth prompted the cruel tyrant Herod the Great to massacre innocent babies in the town of Bethlehem because that was where the prophet Micah had prophesied the Child would be born. The murders of all those precious and innocent infants fulfilled another chilling prophecy:

> A voice was heard in Ramah, Lamentation, weeping, and great mourning, Rachel weeping for her children, Refusing to be comforted, Because they were no more (Matthew 2:18).

Where was the perfect peace for the mothers of Bethlehem? Where was it for Mary, the mother of Jesus, when a sword pierced her soul at her Son's death (Luke 2:35)? Where is it today when mothers' hearts are broken by grief and loss? The sad truth is that such peace will never be found *in this world*. Jesus acknowledged that fact, saying, "Do not think that I came to bring peace on earth. I did not come to bring peace but a sword" (Matthew 10:34).

The peace Jesus brought was of a different sort than some were expecting. In John 14:27, He described it this way: "Peace I leave with you, My peace I give to you; not as the world gives do I give to you. Let not your heart be troubled, neither let it be afraid." His perfect peace would come to dwell within the hearts of His disciples and would fill the early church with boldness in the face of persecution.

The Problem of Suffering

It was necessary for God's Son to know suffering so that He could identify with ordinary people. The Hebrews writer wrote about the things Jesus endured, pointing out that they were for our benefit:

> For we do not have a High Priest who cannot sympathize with our weaknesses, but was in all points tempted as we are, yet without sin (Hebrews 4:15).

> Though He was a Son, yet He learned obedience by the things which He suffered. And having been perfected, He became the author of eternal salvation to all who obey him (Hebrews 5:8-9).

In the hours before His death, Jesus was in anguish. His sweat fell to the ground as great drops of blood (Luke 22:44), and He prayed with "vehement cries and tears to Him who was able to save Him from death" (Hebrews 5:7). Nevertheless, He submitted to the Father's will, saying, "[N]ot as I will, but as You will" (Matthew 26:39). He endured the cross because He was able to look beyond it and see the bigger picture. The Hebrews writer said, "[Look] unto Jesus ... who for the joy that was set before Him endured the cross, despising the shame, and has sat down at the right hand of the throne of God" (12:2).

How we long to experience a peace so strong that it could carry us through our own valleys of depression. We wonder – does such a peace exist?

No God, No Peace

Sept. 11, 2001, was one of those valleys. On that day some 3,000 unsuspecting people in this country died from terrorist attacks, proving that life is uncertain and disaster can strike any of us without warning. It happened that way for the patriarch Job, a righteous man who worshiped God.

People sometimes question how men can believe in a loving God who would allow pain and suffering to exist in the world. They reason that if God is real, He must be incapable of preventing evil. Otherwise, they argue, He is simply unwilling to prevent it, thus proving that He is not a *loving* God after all. By this kind of reasoning, skeptics attempt to make the case that a just and caring Creator does not exist.

But we were created by God in His image as intelligent beings with the ability to reason and make choices. The fact that suffering exists serves to illustrate that point. People can choose to be guided by evil rather than Truth. If they choose not to live by the rules of peace, they create problems for themselves and others.

Isaiah wrote that such people are like the waves of the sea, always tossing up refuse and mud. "There is no peace," said God, "for the wicked" (Isaiah 57:20-21).

> Their works are works of iniquity, And the act of violence is in their hands. Their feet run to evil, And they make haste to shed innocent blood; Their thoughts are thoughts of iniquity; Wasting and destruction are in their paths. The way of peace they have not known, And there is no justice in their ways (59:6-8).

Wicked people are still with us. Motivated by violence and terror, they attempt to undermine the peace that others enjoy, thereby making the world a dangerous place.

In words we have come to love, C.B. McAfee described the only haven where true peace exists:

> *There is a place of quiet rest, near to the heart of God;*
> *A place where sin cannot molest, near to the heart of God.*
> *O Jesus, blest Redeemer, sent from the heart of God,*
> *Hold us who wait before Thee, near to the heart of God.*[3]

Know God, Know Peace

The world is shrinking. With so many different beliefs and practices, how can our many cultures ever hope to coexist peacefully? For some, the answer is pluralism. Pluralism is a "live and let live" approach that accepts all belief systems as equal: "You have your truth; I have mine." This view contradicts biblical teaching that it was God's eternal plan to reconcile people to Himself *through the cross of Christ* (Colossians 1:20).

In the first century it was the gospel that "preach[ed] peace through Jesus Christ" and broke down enmity between Jew and Gentile (Acts 10:36).

> For He Himself [Jesus Christ] is our peace, who has made both one, and has broken down the middle wall of separation, having abolished in His flesh the enmity, that is, the law of commandments contained in ordinances, so as to create in Himself one new man from the two, thus making peace (Ephesians 2:14-15).

Some religions want to eliminate those who disagree with them. Only the gospel can hope to bring people of all backgrounds together as one through a message of love.

The Recipe

The peace of God requires a divine recipe. In this study we will search the Scriptures for the ingredients needed and the instructions provided in His Word. Each chapter will include questions to chew on and a passage to provide food for thought throughout the week. Our world is hungry for peace; the recipe is free, and God wants us to share it.

Questions to Chew On

1. Discuss the implications of Ecclesiastes 1:9. Is this encouraging or discouraging?

2. What is the most difficult challenge you have ever faced? That your parents faced? That your children are likely to face?

3. Does suffering disprove the existence of God?

4. How did Isaiah account for violence in the world (Isaiah 59:6-8)?

5. Is "world peace" possible militarily?

6. What is the source of perfect peace according to Isaiah 26:3?

7. How can people of different backgrounds come together in perfect peace?

8. Read God's invitation, extended in Isaiah 55:1-2, 12. List four points you can learn from this reading.

9. What is "pluralism"?

10. What was Isaiah's recipe for perfect peace (26:3)?

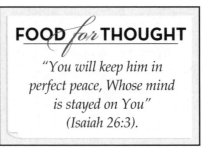

FOOD for THOUGHT

*"You will keep him in
perfect peace, Whose mind
is stayed on You"*
(Isaiah 26:3).

TAKE OUT

If you can't find peace within yourself,
it is useless to seek it elsewhere.

PRAYER *List*

_____

_____

_____

_____

_____

_____

_____

_____

_____

_____

_____

_____

_____

_____

_____

_____

SUBSTITUTIONS

Substituting ingredients in recipes can be tricky. A change in the given ingredients can result in disappointing results, but here are a few substitutions that will generally work.[1]

1 teaspoon allspice = ½ teaspoon cinnamon plus ½ teaspoon cloves

1 teaspoon baking powder = ¼ teaspoon baking powder plus ⅝ teaspoon cream of tartar; or ¼ teaspoon baking soda plus ½ cup buttermilk, sour milk or yogurt (decrease liquid in recipe by ½ cup); or ¼ teaspoon baking soda plus ½ table-spoon vinegar or lemon juice with sweet milk to make ½ cup (decrease liquid in recipe by ½ cup); or ¼ teaspoon baking soda plus ¼ to ½ cup molasses (decrease liquid in recipe by 1-2 tablespoons)

1 cup self-rising flour = 1 cup minus 2 teaspoons all-purpose flour plus 1½ teaspoons baking powder plus dash of salt

1 cup honey = 1¼ cups sugar plus ¼ cup liquid from recipe

1 cup buttermilk = 1 cup minus 1 tablespoon sweet milk plus 1 tablespoon lemon juice or vinegar (let stand 5–10 minutes); or 1 cup sweet milk plus 1¾ teaspoons cream of tartar

1 can sweetened condensed milk = ⅓ cup plus 2 tablespoons

evaporated milk, or 1 cup sugar and 3 tablespoons butter or margarine heated until sugar dissolves and butter dissolves

1 tablespoon yeast = 1 cake yeast, compressed (⅗ ounce); or 1 package (¼ ounce) active dry yeast

1 cup butter = ⅞ to 1 cup hydrogenated fat plus ½ teaspoon salt; or ⅞ cup oil plus ½ teaspoon salt; or ⅞ cup lard plus ½ teaspoon salt; 1 cup margarine; or ⅞ cup oil

1 cup corn syrup = 1 cup sugar plus ¼ cup liquid (same as recipe); or 1 cup honey

1 tablespoon cornstarch = 2 tablespoons all-purpose flour or 4-6 teaspoons quick-cooking tapioca

1 cup sour cream = ⅞ cup sour milk or buttermilk plus ⅓ cup butter or margarine

½ teaspoon cream of tartar = 1½ teaspoons lemon juice or vinegar

1 whole egg (3 tablespoons) = ¼ cup egg substitute

1 egg = 2 egg whites (may add 1-3 teaspoons vegetable oil for each yolk omitted, or 1 egg white plus 2¼ teaspoons non-fat dry milk powder and 2 teaspoons vegetable oil)

CHAPTER 2

THE RECIPE

My mother was a good cook. That's probably why so many family photos capture friends and relatives gathered around our dining table. Many of Mom's recipes – some torn from the newspaper or scrawled on the backs of envelopes – were kept in a kitchen drawer. Others were dog-eared in the half-dozen or so cookbooks sitting on top of the refrigerator in her kitchen.

My mother-in-law had only one cookbook that I remember, but that is because most of her recipes were stored in her head. Mawmaw specialized in dishes she had practiced to the point of perfection. My mouth waters as I think about the cornbread, pot roast, potato salad, collard greens and chocolate pie that one mother or the other was known for. Both moms got excellent training from their mothers who were good cooks, and practice made perfect!

Most of us who like to cook probably learned how in the same way – by watching someone else and following their directions. This is how we become adept at most any skill. We listen and watch; we learn and borrow.

Paul wrote to the church at Philippi with this instruction: "The things which you learned and received and heard and saw in me, these do, and the God of peace will be with you (Philippians 4:9). Paul was imitating Christ, and he encouraged others to follow his example.

Paul dealt with many difficult things. While in Macedonia he experienced fears and conflicts (2 Corinthians 7:5). During his journeys he endured beatings, shipwrecks, attacks and other perils along with weariness, hunger and discomforts of every kind (11:24-27). Yet his writings are filled with many references to the peace he had come to know and wanted to share with others.

Who Needs a Recipe?

Our English word "recipe" comes from the Latin word *recipere*, which means "to receive." Today we think of a recipe as a list of materials and directions for preparing a dish, but at one time the term meant a prescription for medicine. A recipe can also be a procedure for how to do something.

The Bible is a collection of recipes. Its pages are filled with detailed instructions. Some of them teach us how to worship. Others tell us how to treat other people and how to conduct our personal affairs. Some instructions are general in nature, and others are directed to specific individuals or groups. For example:

- God gave Noah a verbal blueprint for the ark that he was to build. God told him explicitly, "[T]his is how you shall make it" (Genesis 6:15).

- The Law of Moses provided details about everyday living that governed the Israelites as a nation. God told Moses, "I will give you tablets of stone, and the law and commandments which I have written, that you may teach them" (Exodus 24:12).

- Repeatedly, God emphasized that all the items in the tabernacle of worship were to be built according to His specific pattern, saying, "And see to it that you make them according to the pattern which was shown you on the mountain"

(Exodus 25:40; 39:42-43; Numbers 8:4. See also Acts 7:44 and Hebrews 8:5).

- Those who dared to alter God's clear instructions were dealt with severely. God considered it "presumptuous" for individuals to tamper with His directives, as in the case of Nadab and Abihu (Leviticus 10:1-3); King Saul (1 Samuel 15:23); King Jeroboam (1 Kings 12:25-30) and Uzzah (2 Samuel 6:7). *touched the ark*

fire

✓ Throughout the Scripture, God consistently warned against the sin of adding to or taking away from His instructions:

- To the Israelite people He said, "You shall not add to the word which I command you, nor take from it, that you may keep the commandments of the Lord your God which I command you" (Deuteronomy 4:2; 12:32).

- The Proverbs also contain this admonition. "Do not add to His words, Lest He reprove you, and you be found a liar" (Proverbs 30:6).

- A similar warning accompanied the Holy Spirit's revelation to John. "For I testify to everyone who hears the words of the prophecy of this book: If anyone adds to these things, God will add to him the plagues that are written in this book; and if anyone takes away from the words of the book of this prophecy, God shall take away his part from the Book of Life, from the holy city, and from the things which are written in this book" (Revelation 22:18-19).

Why do human beings need a book of instructions? Because our own know-how is limited. The prophet Jeremiah wrote, "O Lord, I know the way of man is not in himself; It is not in man who walks to direct his own steps" (10:23). Proverbs 3:5-6 advises, "Trust in the Lord with all your heart, And lean not on your own understanding; In all your ways acknowledge Him, And He shall direct your paths." Solomon learned firsthand that "[t]here is a way that seems right to a man, But its end is the way of death" (Proverbs 14:12). Living according to God's laws will result in peace of mind, according to Psalm 119:165.

David recognized that the word of the Lord is "proven" (Psalm 18:30). This means it has been tested and shown to be reliable. The wisdom found in the Bible can be counted upon to guide people (Psalm 119:130). God's instructions need no alterations as given. We should not attempt to change them to suit our tastes or preferences.

What About Substitutions?

I've enjoyed ribbing my husband about something he did years ago when we were newly married. In the middle of making a chocolate cake, I realized I was out of cocoa. Being the helpful mate that he is (and loving chocolate), he volunteered to make a run to the grocery for more. He returned with a can of instant cocoa mix, the kind used to make hot chocolate. Our conversation went something like this:

"Did you get the cocoa?"

"Uh-huh."

"This isn't cocoa."

"Why not? It says cocoa on the label."

"What I need is plain cocoa. This is a mix. It won't work."

We laughed, but needless to say, making that cake required another trip to the store. And that's the trouble with substitutions – they often don't work, as with the account of Nadab and Abihu, recorded in Leviticus 10. Their exchange may have gone like this:

"Did you bring the fire for the incense?"

"Here it is."

"Did you get it from the altar?"

"What difference does it make? Fire is fire."

You probably know how that turned out. By substituting their own choice of fire, they demonstrated that they did not regard God's instructions as important (Leviticus 10:3). Treating His command with disrespect was the essence of presumptuous sin, condemned repeatedly in Scripture.

People today often feel comfortable making changes where God has given specific instructions. But when it comes to obedience, one course of action is not as good as another. The Bible is filled with examples that make this point.

> For whatever things were written before were written for our learning, that we through the patience and comfort of the Scriptures might have hope (Romans 15:4).

> Now all these things [Israel's punishments] happened to them as examples, and they were written for our admonition, upon whom the ends of the ages have come (1 Corinthians 10:11).

Is the Bible Outdated?

I saved many of my mother's cookbooks after she died. Several of them contained "old timey" recipes from the Shakers or the Amish. One book even has recipes from the Civil War era. These old recipes are interesting, but some would be difficult to follow today because they are outdated. Some require hard-to-find ingredients or a method of preparation that simply isn't practical.

One of these recipes is for "syllabub," a drink that was popular in the 1800s. It calls for cider sweetened with crushed maple sugar and topped with nutmeg. According to the directions, adding milk directly from the cow will produce a drink that is warm and foamy!

Fortunately, cooking has changed a great deal since the days of our great-grandmothers. Today we have more modern appliances and ingredients from around the world that we didn't have to grow ourselves. And aren't we glad?

Some people view the Bible this way – as an outdated book. They may hold on to it for sentimental reasons, just as I keep my mom's old cookbooks in my cupboard. But they also consider the Bible's teachings to be irrelevant and unnecessary for today's world. Activities the Scriptures call immoral, therefore, are considered acceptable to many. Virtue is old-fashioned, forbearance is for the weak and submission is a patriarchal concept that the church has outgrown. And when it comes to doctrine, many churchgoers expect sermons designed to entertain rather than teach.

Psalm 119:160 talks about the enduring quality of God's Word. David wrote in Psalm 19:7-11:

> The law of the Lord is perfect, converting the soul; The testimony of the Lord is sure, making wise the simple; The statutes of the Lord are right, rejoicing the heart; The commandment of the Lord is pure, enlightening the eyes; The fear of the Lord is clean, enduring forever; The judgments of the Lord are true and righteous altogether. More to be desired are they than gold, Yea, than much fine gold; Sweeter also than honey and the honeycomb. Moreover by them Your servant is warned, And in keeping them there is great reward.

Notice the benefits of His Word that are named here. It is good for the soul, the heart and the eyes; and like honey, it sweetens life. It is true that God required some things of people living before the Christian era that He no longer requires of people today. Likewise, there are new commandments meant just for Christians. But the principles of right living found in the Bible are not outdated. They can still satisfy those who are spiritually hungry (Psalm 107:9).

A Spiritual Appetite

Long ago David wrote about the marvelous design of the human body, saying, "I am fearfully and wonderfully made" (Psalm 139:14). The way our body systems work together to maintain good health is amazing. The average body consumes an estimated 40 tons of food in a lifetime.[2] Feeding this human machine is a never-ending task, and we would grow tired of doing it if we were not equipped with a healthy appetite. So our bodies send out hunger pangs when they are not getting the nourishment they need.

Cravings, however, can be evidence of an unbalanced system. They can serve as a signal that some need is not being satisfied. If we have consumed a steady diet of junk food, for example, craving a home-cooked meal may be the body's way of letting us know we are not getting proper nourishment. A poor appetite can also mean that something is wrong with the body. Within the soul is a spiritual appetite that needs to be fed. It sends us signals, too. A case in point is that of Solomon, who became rich and famous but in the process neglected the spiritual nourishment he had received as a young man. He became empty and tried to satisfy his spiritual hunger with things that could not fill the need. The book of Ecclesiastes tells how he attempted to fill the void with learning, pleasure and material objects. These, incidentally, are the same tidbits that Satan dangles before each one of us (1 John 2:16).

Solomon developed a kind of spiritual gluttony, writing later, "Whatever my eyes desired I did not keep from them. I did not withhold my heart from any pleasure" (Ecclesiastes 2:10). Unhealthy cravings had created an insatiable appetite that all of his riches could not fill. Neglecting his spiritual needs left him hating life because all his efforts to find peace were futile – a "grasping for the wind" (v. 17). Eventually, Solomon realized his error and concluded that the "whole" of every man – or that which applies to every man – is this: to "[f]ear God and keep His commandments" (12:13).

Submitting to God's plan is the only avenue to spiritual peace, and this is exactly what God stressed to Solomon as a young man (1 Chronicles 28:9). Solomon knew what God's law required, but he learned the hard way that substituting our will for God's brings sorrow.

Consuming More and Enjoying It Less

Like King Solomon, many people today are struggling to satisfy an unhealthy appetite. Gregg Easterbrook has written that our generation should be enjoying life more than our forefathers did because of our affluence. We enjoy good health care, more leisure time and the advances in technology that have made life better in so many ways. In his 2004 book, *The Progress Paradox: How Life Gets Better While People Feel Worse*, he suggests that this is not the case.[3] For many people today, prosperity has not resulted in peace of mind.

Our souls *need* the spiritual sustenance that only Jesus can provide.

> I am the bread of life. He who comes to Me shall never hunger, and he who believes in Me shall never thirst … This is the bread which comes down out of heaven, that one may eat of it and not die. I am the living bread which came down from heaven. If anyone eats of this bread, he will live forever; and the bread that I shall give is My flesh, which I shall give for the life of the world (John 6:35, 50-51).

Spiritual Vitamins

According to Philippians 4:7, the peace that God can provide serves as a guard for our hearts and minds. The Greek word used here for "guard," *phroureo*, is a military term. It signifies that we are garrisoned or protected by His peace.[4] Much like an antioxidant that protects the body from disease, the peace of God strengthens the Christian against many spiritual diseases, such as those listed in Galatians 5:19-21.

S.I. McMillen, author of the 1993 best-seller *None of These Diseases*, put it this way:

> Peace does not come in capsules! This is regrettable because medical science recognizes that emotions such as fear, sorrow, envy, resentment and hatred are responsible for the majority of our sicknesses.[5]

Although peace cannot be bought in tablet form, a sure remedy exists within the Word of God for the troubled soul. Using its proven prescriptions, we can protect our hearts while adding length of days and quality to our lives.

Questions to Chew On

1. What is a recipe, literally?

2. How do you decide if a recipe is trustworthy?

3. In what way is the Bible like a collection of recipes?

4. Give some examples from Scripture of God's specific instructions that were not to be altered.

5. What is presumptuous sin?

6. Discuss some things to which people often turn for support when they are troubled.

7. How would you reason with someone who claims the Bible is outdated?

8. How is it that Solomon, the richest and most powerful man of his day, came to hate life?

9. Many physical and emotional problems have spiritual causes. Discuss what some of these might be.

10. How does peace serve as a spiritual "guard" for our hearts and minds (Philippians 4:7)?

FOOD for THOUGHT

"Do not be wise in your own eyes; Fear the Lord and depart from evil. It will be health to your flesh, And strength to your bones" (Proverbs 3:7-8).

TAKE OUT

The Bible contains the vitamins for a healthy soul.
A chapter a day keeps Satan away.

PRAYER *List*

A FAVORITE RECIPE

Trusted recipes are often cherished. You can refer to them over and over, and generally the results will always turn out the same. Almost everyone has several of these. You've used them so often that you have them memorized, and they have become your signature contributions at church suppers and family get-togethers. Perhaps they were passed down from a previous generation, or you may have stumbled across them in a cookbook or magazine. One of my favorite recipes for yeast rolls is below.

While waiting for the dough to rise, spend some time thinking about a favorite Bible passage that serves as "soul food" for you.

Butterhorn Rolls

Ingredients
   1 cup milk
   ½ cup butter-flavored shortening
   1 package active dry yeast
   ½ cup sugar
   1 teaspoon salt
   3 eggs, beaten
   4 cups bread flour, sifted
   melted butter
   softened butter

Directions

In a small saucepan, scald the milk. Remove the pan from the heat, and pour the milk over the shortening in a large bowl. Combine the yeast and sugar in a small bowl, and stir to mix. When the milk mixture is lukewarm, add the yeast mixture. Stir with a whisk. Add the salt and the beaten eggs, stirring with a whisk after each addition. Add the flour slowly, and mix it in with a large, non-metal spoon.

Let the dough rise until double in size, about 1½ to 2 hours, or cover and place in the refrigerator overnight. Divide the dough into two sections. On a floured surface, roll out each section with a rolling pin into about a 10-inch circle. Brush with melted butter.

Grease a baking sheet with softened butter. Cut each section of dough into 12 or more wedges. Roll up each wedge, starting with the wide end, as you would a crescent roll. Place on the prepared pan 1 inch apart, and let them rise again; or, if not using immediately, put back into the refrigerator and bring out to rise for about 2 hours before baking. Bake rolls at 375 degrees for 10 to 12 minutes. Brush with melted butter. Yield: 24 rolls.

CHAPTER 3

COOKING WITH PAUL

Most women have favorite recipes. Sometimes they are handed down through generations, and sometimes they are brand new. In recent years, experts like Paula Deen from The Food Network have helped a whole generation of women to develop their culinary skills through their writings and video presentations. Paula's Southern Fried Chicken continues to be a favorite.

Just as we have favorite foods we enjoy eating, many of us also have favorite passages of Scripture. These verses serve as *spiritual* comfort food when our souls are hungry for nourishment. One of my personal favorites is Philippians 4:4-9. This passage is, in essence, a spiritual recipe, straight from the pen of Paul (not Paula). I have come to think of it as one of Paul's favorites because it calls for some spiritual ingredients he uses often.

The remainder of our study will focus on this beautiful recipe, with the hope that it will come to be one of your favorites as well. But before we look at Paul's recipe for peace, it will be helpful to study the background of the book of Philippians.

The Church at Philippi

Luke, the author of Acts, suggested that the congregation at Philippi was the first church of Christ on European soil. It was established by Paul and others during his second missionary journey after the apostle saw a vision of a man from Macedonia standing and pleading, "Come over to Macedonia and help us" (Acts 16:9). Among the first to obey the gospel in that city were Lydia, a wealthy merchant woman, and a jailer who is unnamed. Both were baptized into Christ along with their households (vv. 10-40).

A special bond developed between Paul and the congregation at Philippi, perhaps because of the persecution he and Silas experienced while there. In the years that followed, this church repeatedly sent Paul financial support, and the fact that they were the only church that did shows just how much they valued his friendship (Philippians 1:3-5; 4:15). It was the providence of God that brought Paul to Philippi the first time, but it was their mutual love that returned him on several occasions.

Time passed, perhaps a decade or so, and Paul was transported to Rome to stand trial for his preaching. He spent two years in the city, chained and under house arrest (Acts 28:30). When the Philippians heard about his plight, they sent a messenger named Epaphroditus to carry a contribution to him and to inquire about his welfare (Philippians 4:17-18; also 2:25).

We can picture just how touched Paul must have been as he dictated a reply. The plan, he told them, was to send Epaphroditus back to them and that Timothy also would leave for Philippi as soon as Paul got word about his appeal. Believing he would be exonerated and released, Paul also prepared for a possible sentence of death (Philippians 1:20-21). Remarkably, he was at peace with whatever the verdict would be.

A Troubled Congregation

Meanwhile, the Christians at Philippi were experiencing problems, too. They were worried about the man who was their father in the faith. They knew about the incident when Paul and Silas were imprisoned in their city for casting a spirit of divination out of a young woman (Acts 16). They understood the cost of discipleship that Paul had paid through the years. Now he was imprisoned again, and following this verdict no further appeal would be possible.

Paul's suffering foreshadowed a growing hostility toward Christians everywhere, and others could expect to experience similar persecution. Paul hinted at this in Philippians 1:27-30, where he urged the church to strive together for the faith. He hoped to hear that they had not been terrified by their adversaries and reminded them that they must be ready to suffer for Christ's sake also.

False teachers were another problem, threatening the unity of the church in many places. Some encouraged immorality with their loose living and preaching. Others, those of the circumcision, demanded that Gentile Christians adopt Jewish rites and practices. Paul told the Philippians to be wary of both kinds of teachers who were circulating these divisive doctrines (Philippians 3:1-2).

The problems of first-century churches did not come only from outside their fellowship. Many times the problems were internal. It seemed that a faction was developing within the congregation at Philippi. Paul alluded to it when he appealed to them to be like-minded, having a common love, being of one accord and one mind (Philippians 2:2). He reminded them to guard against selfish ambition or conceit and urged them to be lowly of mind, esteeming others better than themselves (v. 3). He warned about the problems that murmuring and disputing can create (v. 14). Although the real source of the problem at Philippi was not spelled out, two women clearly were contributing to it. Euodia and Syntyche, whatever their disagreement, were not "of the same mind in the Lord" (4:2). Their disagreement had the potential to disrupt the peace and harmony of this good congregation.

On top of everything else, the church was now worried about its messenger, Epaphroditus. News had reached them that he had become ill, and in fact he had nearly died (Philippians 2:25-27). There seemed to be problems on top of problems for this congregation of God's people. If anyone needed encouragement, this body of believers certainly did.

Paul's Reply

In this epistle, Paul set out to relieve the Philippian church's fears. One by one, he addressed their concerns and guided them in dealing with their anxieties. As for his personal welfare, he assured them that his imprisonment had turned out for good because God, in His great providence, had answered Paul's prayers in an unexpected way. Having planned to visit Rome for years (Acts 19:21), Paul had been given a free ticket and a captive audience for his message. Because of his chains, the whole palace guard had the opportunity to hear his story, and in the process they learned about Christ (Philippians 1:13). A positive attitude if ever there was one!

Concerning the persecution some of these Christians had yet to undergo, Paul reminded the Philippians that it would serve as proof of their salvation (Philippians 1:28-29). By consenting to let God work within their lives, they were privileged to have a part in their salvation (2:12-13). As a result, they would "shine as lights in the world" (v. 15). It was a reminder, perhaps, of Jesus' teaching that He is "the light of the world" (John 8:12) and that His followers must "[l]et your light so shine before men, that they may see your good works and glorify your Father in heaven" (Matthew 5:16). Such confidence would go a long way in offsetting the fear of persecution by mere mortals.

Paul also relieved their concerns for Epaphroditus. The good brother had recovered, Paul told them. He gave God the credit for raising him up, assuring them that he was returning home and should be received with gladness (Philippians 2:27-29).

Concerning false teachers, Paul assured his readers that they must not be intimidated by the Jews among them who put their confidence in a fleshly pedigree. The loss of material wealth or position is nothing compared to the excellence of the knowledge of Christ. Whatever one might sacrifice on His behalf is rubbish compared to the prize that comes from faith in Jesus (Philippians 3:8-9).

Finally, addressing the disunity that had threatened to divide the church, Paul tackled it head-on, calling the instigators by name and gently appealing to them to work out their differences. He reminded them that their names were written among others' in the Book of Life – a subtle admonition, perhaps, about what was at stake if they continued to be at odds (Philippians 4:2-3).

The Recipe for Peace

In Philippians 4:4-9, Paul concluded his peaceful appeal with what is perhaps the most beautiful section of his epistle. Herein is a checklist for how one can experience a peace so surpassing in understanding that it can fortify the heart and mind against whatever threats Satan might devise (v. 7). Paul wrote:

Rejoice in the Lord always. Again I will say, rejoice! Let your gentleness be known to all men. The Lord is at hand. Be anxious for nothing, but in everything by prayer and supplication, with thanksgiving, let your requests be made known to God; and the peace of God, which surpasses all understanding, will guard your hearts and minds through Christ Jesus. Finally, brethren, whatever things are true, whatever things are noble, whatever things are just, whatever things are pure, whatever things are lovely, whatever things are of good report, if there is any virtue and if there is anything praiseworthy – meditate on these things. The things which you learned and received and heard and saw in me, these do, and the God of peace will be with you (Philippians 4:4-9).

These words reveal a confidence born out of spiritual maturity. Paul wanted his readers to acquire the same measure of maturity that had emboldened him (Philippians 3:15), which means that Christians today can enjoy the same promise. We, too, can come to know the peace that passes understanding (4:7).

Put the Recipe to Work

The Bible sometimes leaves us with unanswered questions. Did the church at Philippi rejoice to hear that Paul might be released? Did they grow stronger, resolving to accept whatever persecution might come their way? Did they urge Euodia and Syntyche to mend their differences? Was the congregation blessed with a new sense of unity, becoming a kinder and gentler body in the process?

The entire book of Philippians can be read in less than half an hour and is so practical in tone that it is easy to digest. The book has much to offer us as women living in the 21st century. The fact is that we wrestle with many of the same issues as our sisters living in ancient Philippi. We worry about the welfare of those we love. Our personal faith comes under attack at times, and we are challenged to defend it to unbelievers. We've experienced doctrinal divisions and the problems they create within the church. We see a need to fortify our children against false teaching when it arises. And when it comes to church problems, we must admit that they still happen and often stem from personality differences – with women sometimes at the forefront!

In her book *Shine Like Stars*, Dolly Leighton has this to say:

> Philippians is a letter that a Christian woman can truly take to heart. Paul teaches that all I do on the job, at home and in the community must be tempered with love, joy, peace, gentleness and humility. I must show that God works in me to will and to act according to His purpose (Philippians 2:13). I must show that Christ lives in me every day and in every way. Keeping Paul's words to the Philippians continuously before me is a way of tempering my will to His will. Only then will I shine like a star holding out the Word of Life.[1]

The book of Philippians contains a recipe for peace that just may become one of your favorites. Read Philippians 4:4-9 again, and underline each ingredient you see that you will need. Jot them down on a list; then grab an apron and the Book, and together let's create something worth tasting and sharing with others.

Questions to Chew On

1. Review the first part of Paul's second missionary journey (Acts 16:1-12). How did he come to preach in Philippi?

2. Think of a time or times when the providence of God has brought you into contact with people who have greatly impacted your life. How was that true in Paul's case?

3. Had Paul been focused upon his problems, what were some things he could have shared with the Philippian brethren (see again 2 Corinthians 11:24-28)? What was his attitude, as recorded in Philippians 2:4?

4. How was this attitude characteristic of Christ (Philippians 2:5-8)?

5. In pointing the brethren to Christ, what message did Paul drive home in Philippians 2:14?

6. What was Paul's attitude about his own mistreatment, including his chains (Philippians 1:12-18)?

7. Is persecution a concern for Christians today? When it happens, should we be surprised (2 Timothy 3:12)?

8. Of the problems faced at Philippi, which do you believe are most common in churches today?

9. Do you ever become discouraged as a Christian? What discourages you most?

10. Name a scripture that comforts you when you are down.

FOOD for THOUGHT

"Therefore do not worry about tomorrow, for tomorrow will worry about its own things. Sufficient for the day is its own trouble" (Matthew 6:34).

TAKE OUT

Feed your faith, and doubt will starve to death.

PRAYER *List*

TIMELESS INGREDIENTS

Bread, often called "the staff of life," has been a staple of the human diet since the earliest times. Women today prepare it with many of the same basic ingredients used by our ancient ancestors. Most bread is made from a grain of some type; milk, cream or some other liquid; a leavening agent; and fat or oil. Sometimes nuts, salt, eggs and sweeteners such as fruit or honey are added to improve the taste and texture.

The following recipe, dubbed "Scripture Bread" has been around for a long time. We've done the research for you and can vouch for the taste – it's delicious! As you sample it, be reminded that God's truths, like these ingredients, are timeless and available to people in every generation.

Scripture Bread

Ingredients
1 cup of Proverbs 30:33 (butter)
2 cups of Judges 14:18 (honey, although I recommend sugar*)
6 of Isaiah 10:14 (eggs)
½ cup of Judges 4:19 (milk)
2 tablespoons of 1 Samuel 14:25 (honey)
4 cups of 1 Kings 4:22 (plain flour)
A pinch of Leviticus 2:13 (salt)

1 teaspoon of Exodus 30:23 (spices – cinnamon works well)
2 teaspoons of Amos 4:5 (leavening or baking powder)
2 cups of Proverbs 25:11 (apples), chopped
2 cups of 1 Samuel 25:18 (figs, raisins or dates)
2 cups of Numbers 17:8 (almonds or other nuts)

If using honey, use ¾ cup of honey to replace 1 cup sugar. Reduce other liquids by about ½ cup for each cup of honey added.

Directions

Preheat the oven to 350 degrees. Grease and flour 8 mini-loaf pans. Cream together one cup (2 sticks) of butter and 2 cups of sugar. Beat 6 eggs in a separate bowl until frothy, and then add milk and honey; set aside. Sift flour, salt, cinnamon and baking powder in another bowl. Add flour mixture alternating with egg mixture to the creamed butter mixture, beginning and ending with flour mixture. Mix until just blended. Next add chopped apples, figs, raisins or dates, and nuts to the batter. Fold ingredients carefully. Pour into greased and floured mini-pans. Bake at 350 degrees for 30 minutes or until inserted toothpick comes out clean. Yield: 8 mini-loaves.

CHAPTER 4

STOCK YOUR
SPIRITUAL PANTRY

Spiritual maturity should be the goal of every Christian. "Brethren, do not be children in understanding … in malice be babes, but in understanding be mature," Paul wrote in 1 Corinthians 14:20. Developing maturity as a Christian takes time and a great deal of practice, just like becoming a really good cook. We certainly will not reach that goal overnight. And like all who are dedicated to becoming expert cooks, we should constantly be honing our craft, hoping to learn something new to improve our skills. But the quest for spiritual maturity (which Paul called a transformation of our minds in Romans 12:2) is worth the effort it requires.

Paul understood what a transformation involves. In his letter to the Philippians, he mentioned things he had given up for the sake of serving Christ Jesus. Compared to the prize that awaited him, he viewed them all as insignificant – his former accomplishments as mere status symbols that were important only by worldly standards (Philippians 3:5; 4:12). This amazing attitude reveals that he was learning to think like Christ. So he encouraged the Philippians, "Let this mind be *in you* which was also in Christ Jesus" (2:5, emphasis added). He went on to remind them about everything Christ gave up when He came to do the Father's will. Later he repeated, "[L]et us, *as many as are mature*, have this mind" (3:15, emphasis added).

How do we, as ordinary Christian women, develop this spiritual maturity that Paul said we must? How does any woman learn to cook? She reads, reads, reads – but that isn't all. She is constantly practicing – following the directions and learning from her mistakes. It shouldn't be any surprise that we develop spiritual maturity in the same way.

In Ephesians 4:13-14, Paul pointed to the Word of God as the source that can help us grow up into Christ and become mature like Him. In a similar vein, he told the Colossians to be "filled with the knowledge of [Christ's] will in all wisdom and spiritual understanding," the goal being that each may become perfect (or mature) in Christ (Colossians 1:9; 28). As we grow in our goal of thinking like Jesus, a wonderful thing happens. Paul said the peace of God comes to rule in our hearts (Colossians 3:15).

Think Like Christ

Our transformation begins as we learn to control the way we think. Does that sound easy? It isn't! That's because the way we think is controlled by the attitudes we form early in life. Those attitudes become the staple ingredients of the life we create. We've all heard the adage, "You are what you eat." We could just as easily say, "You are what you think." This very thing is taught in Proverbs 23:7, which teaches that "as [a man] thinks in his heart, so is he." Developing spiritual maturity – which leads to peace – starts with the right attitudes.

Depending upon the particular "scripture recipe" we consult, a list of necessary ingredients might be love, joy, peace, long-suffering, kindness, goodness, faithfulness, gentleness and self-control (Galatians 5:22-23). Another "recipe" lists faith, virtue (moral excellence), knowledge, self-control, perseverance, godliness, brotherly kindness and love (2 Peter 1:5-7). Wherever we are in our Christian development, it is important to take stock periodically to determine whether we are growing in these attitudes. It may help to think of our hearts as spiritual pantries in which we store the things we need in order to grow up into Christ.

The young Christian is much like a new bride. (The church is pictured as the bride of Christ in passages such as John 3:29; Ephesians 5:24 and Revelation 21:9.) Because she is just starting out, it's understandable that it may take time for her to fill her cupboard with all the essentials. But what about those of us who have been at it for years? What do our spiritual pantries look like? Maybe it's time to take stock.

The Right Spiritual Ingredients

According to Webster, an "attitude" is a way of acting, feeling or thinking that reveals one's disposition. A close inspection of our heart will reveal the attitudes we are working with. Proverbs 4:23 says, "Watch over your heart with all diligence; For from it flow the springs of life" (NASB). So Paul said, "Examine yourselves" (2 Corinthians 13:5). It's time to open up the doors of our hearts and take inventory. We can no more achieve peace with the wrong attitudes than we can make bread with the wrong ingredients.

Shad Helmstetter, a well-known author and lecturer in the field of motivational behavior, maintains that "attitudes are the filters through which we view everything in our sight." He writes,

> When I was quite young I first heard the Biblical passage which reads, "As a man thinketh, so is he." I recall shaking my head, thinking that could not be. … Little did I (or most of us then) understand that the Biblical passage had hit the nail of truth squarely on the head. It would be years later, however, after much research, and following the discoveries through which modern-day neuroscientists had begun to unlock the secrets of the human mind, that I would come to know just how correct – how *scientifically* correct – that Biblical passage had been.[1]

We will not be ready to acquire the peace of God in our hearts until we have accumulated the attitudes that contribute to it. It is important, then, to take stock of how we think.

Discard the Old

If we take the time to check, we will find that most items in our kitchen cupboards have an expiration date. That date is important because ingredients can lose their effectiveness over time. When that's the case they need to be tossed out because they can even become unhealthy.

Once we become Christians, paying attention to the attitudes we have acquired is just as important. We must rid ourselves of those that are unhealthy. Paul wrote, "When I was a child, I used to speak as a child, think as a child, reason like a child; when I became a man, I did away with childish things" (1 Corinthians 13:11 NASB).

To the Colossians, Paul wrote about putting off the old man (Colossians 3:9). First he enumerated some desires of a sexual nature, such as fornication, uncleanness, passion, etc. He added to the list covetousness, or the desire for things that are not lawful for a person to have. He seemed to indicate that the Christians to whom he was writing were already aware that these things were wrong. These kinds of sins are usually more obvious, so new Christians would have been admonished early on about the need to remove them from their lives. Then Paul added, "But now you yourselves are to put off all these: anger, wrath, malice, blasphemy [slander], filthy language out of your mouth." He went on to include lying (vv. 5-9). Replacing every one of those old habits may take some time and effort.

When throwing out what is bad, it is important to begin replacing it right away with what is good. Paul encouraged his readers to replace their old ways of thinking with compassion, kindness, humility, gentleness, forgiveness and love (Colossians 3:12-15). And the process does take time.

Anger: Use in Moderation

One thing we must use sparingly is anger. We don't necessarily need to throw it out altogether, but frequent use can lead to some serious problems.

Anger is an abiding condition of the mind that often looks toward revenge. It can simmer almost unnoticed. Wrath, on the other hand, is an outburst of feeling that results from anger and is usually spontaneous. Malice stems from a viciousness of character, and it may lead one person to slander another or say hateful and harmful things about

SIMMER

verb – to remain at or just below the boiling point, usually forming tiny bubbles with a low, murmuring sound.

her. These feelings might be accompanied by abusive speech that is foul or filthy, and they might even lead to lying – out and out deception.[2] That is why anger unchecked can be quite harmful.

All anger is not bad, however, and it isn't possible to eliminate it altogether. One can hardly view the senseless violence and evil in the world without a sense of "righteous indignation." The psalmist noted that God is a righteous judge who gets angry at injustice. The King James Version says that "God is angry with the wicked every day" (Psalm 7:11). The Scriptures, in fact, speak about the fierceness of His anger and note that it "burned" (Joshua 7:26; Exodus 4:14 NIV). God's anger, however, always has these characteristics:

• *It is under control.* "But He, being full of compassion, forgave their iniquity, And did not destroy them. Yes, many a time He turned His anger away, And did not stir up all His wrath" (Psalm 78:38).

• *It is always directed toward wrongdoing.* "The Lord is longsuffering and abundant in mercy, forgiving iniquity and transgression; but He by no means clears the guilty" (Numbers 14:18).

• *It is short-lived.* "He will not always strive with us, Nor will He keep His anger forever" (Psalm 103:9).

• *It is always accompanied by a willingness to forgive.* "For You, Lord, are good, and ready to forgive, And abundant in mercy to all those who call upon You" (Psalm 86:5).

Ephesians 4:26 teaches that it is possible for people to become angry without sinning. But Scripture also warns us to be "slow to speak and slow to become angry" (James 1:19 NIV).

Put a Lid on It

Every cook knows that a covered pot reaches the boiling point more quickly than one that is uncovered. Anger that is turned inward and concealed is apt to boil over. So that we don't reach the boiling point, venting our feelings can be a good idea. But remember, a pressure cooker can leave a nasty burn! Experience bears out that venting frustration to the one who has made us angry must be done carefully. Ephesians 4:15 advises that we speak the truth in love.

Bill Flatt, a counseling psychologist, has enumerated some destructive physical and emotional effects of anger turned inward. These include fear, tension, revenge, self-pity, self-destruction, increased blood pressure and heartbeat, blood clots, increased adrenalin, tense muscles, stomach pain, strokes, angina pectoris, heart attacks, headaches, nausea, gastric ulcers, drinking and high cholesterol, among others.[3]

Clearly, we can't fume and find peace of mind. David found this to be true, writing about a time when he was bound up in silence and remained quiet, "with enjoyment gone while my distress grew worse. My heart was hot within me; in my musing the fire burned; I pled with my tongue" (Psalm 39:2-3 MODERN LANGUAGE BIBLE). Anger that is allowed to simmer will eventually boil over and may result in hurt to ourselves and others. We have to wonder, had Euodia and Syntyche spent some time fuming? How might their differences have been resolved in a more effective way?

A Heart Grown Cold

Peace of mind also suffers when hearts grow cold toward God and others. It can happen if we dwell upon past disappointments to the point that bitterness congeals into a kind of rigidity and the heart becomes unresponsive. Jesus warned about this in Matthew 24:12, saying that in difficult times the love of many grows cold. Being able to overcome bitterness is a sign of maturity.

Joseph, whose story is recorded in Genesis 37-45, was one who showed great maturity in this respect. At the age of 17, he was betrayed by his own brothers and carried as a captive into Egypt. Because they resented his favored treatment by their dad, the brothers committed a terrible wrong that they would live to regret deeply (37:4, 11). They vented their anger in a way that caused great injury to Joseph and ultimately to themselves and their father. Later, through the providence of God, Joseph rose to a position of great power in Egypt and could have exacted his revenge upon the brothers. But retaliation would have added even more unhappiness to many lives, including his own. He forgave his brothers' wrongs and treated them kindly. Rather than allow bitterness to overcome him, he chose to "overcome evil with good" (Romans 12:21).

Use the Control Knob

Temperance is one of the attitudes we must acquire as we rid ourselves of destructive kinds of anger. "Temperance," from the Greek *kratos*, means "strength." It is often translated as "self-control," and W.E. Vine suggests that it demands "the controlling power of the will under the operation of the Spirit of God."[4] We might think of temperance as the control knob that regulates the temperature of our hearts. When we recognize that God works providentially in our lives today, just as He did in Joseph's life, it becomes easier to control feelings of resentment. We can rest in confidence, knowing that "all things work together for good to those who love God, to those who are the called according to His purpose" (Romans 8:28).

Joseph came to understand that God had been at work in his life all along, even when things were the most difficult (Genesis 45:5-8). That realization made it easier for him to forgive the brothers who had wronged him. So Joseph named his firstborn son Manasseh – "making to forget" – for, he said, "God has made me forget all my toil and all my father's house" (41:51). Refusing to give in to bitterness kept his heart from growing cold with resentment and resulted in a great blessing.

Time to Take Inventory

For new Christians, the peace of God starts with a personal inventory. (That also applies to those of us who have been in the "kitchen" a long time but have never become serious about "cooking.") Attitudes that are harmful must be discarded to make room for new and healthier ways of thinking. The feelings we bring to stressful situations must be regulated with self-control. Once we determine to make some changes in how we think, we are on our way to experiencing the perfect peace we so desire.

Questions to Chew On

1. What are some characteristics of spiritual maturity?

2. How did Paul define "the mind of Christ" in Philippians 2:5-8?

3. List some basic ingredients needed for creating peace in our lives. Make a personal list of the ones of which your supply is getting short.

4. Define "attitude."

5. Why is it important to keep watch over our hearts?

6. List some attitudes and behaviors that Christians must discard.

7. Discuss the differences between anger, wrath, malice, slander, abusive speech and lying.

8. What are some characteristics of God's anger?

9. What happens when simmering goes unchecked?

10. Why is a cold heart just as dangerous as a hot head?

FOOD *for* THOUGHT

"For as the churning of milk produces butter, And wringing the nose produces blood, So the forcing of wrath produces strife" (Proverbs 30:33).

TAKE OUT

I was angry with my friend;
I told my wrath, my wrath did end.
I was angry with my foe;
I told it not, my wrath did grow.
– William Blake [5]

PRAYER *List*

_____

_____

_____

_____

_____

_____

_____

_____

_____

_____

_____

_____

_____

_____

BAKING BREAD

H ebrew women baked loaves of bread every day except the Sabbath. Most of their bread was made from barley. Jesus once worked a great miracle using a boy's lunch of five barley loaves and two fish (John 6:9), which was probably a fairly typical meal. Flour for more special occasions was made from wheat (Exodus 29:2; Psalm 81:16).

During their wilderness years the Hebrews often dreamed about "a land of wheat and barley" that awaited them in Canaan (Deuteronomy 8:8). They later found that both crops grew extremely well in the Promised Land. Barley ripened in early spring followed by wheat in late May. Early in June the Feast of Weeks, or Pentecost, celebrated the harvest of both with the first loaves of the season being dedicated to God (Leviticus 23).

Making bread in those days was a time-consuming process. (How thankful we should be for our modern kitchens!) Women had to sift the grain with a sieve before grinding it into flour with a stone or a mill. Then salt and water were mixed in, and sometimes oil or honey was added to improve the texture and flavor. Kneading in a piece of fermented dough from a former baking allowed the mixture to rise and become leavened before being baked on a rock or in an oven. After all that work, a hot loaf must have tasted delicious!

Wheat Bread

Ingredients
3 cups warm water (110 degrees)
2 (¼ ounce) packages active dry yeast
⅓ cup honey
5 cups white bread flour
3 tablespoons butter, melted
⅓ cup honey
1 tablespoon salt
3½ cups whole wheat flour
2 tablespoons butter or margarine, melted

Directions
In a large bowl, mix warm water, yeast and ⅓ cup honey. Add 5 cups white bread flour, and stir to combine. Let stand for 30 minutes or until big and bubbly.

Mix in 3 tablespoons melted butter, ⅓ cup honey and salt. Stir in 2 cups whole wheat flour. Flour a flat surface, and knead with whole wheat flour until not very sticky – just pulling away from the counter but still sticky to touch. This may take an additional 2 to 4 cups of whole wheat flour. Place in a greased bowl, turning once to coat the surface of the dough. Cover with a dish towel. Let rise in a warm place until doubled.

Punch down, and divide into 3 loaves. Place in greased 9-by-5-inch loaf pans, and allow to rise until dough has topped the pans by one inch.

Bake at 350 degrees for 25 to 30 minutes; do not overbake. Lightly brush the tops of loaves with 2 tablespoons melted butter or margarine when done to prevent crust from getting hard. Cool completely. Yield: 3 loaves.

CHAPTER 5

FIRST THE JOY

Most recipes consist of a key ingredient, and everything else is there to enhance it. That isn't to say that the other ingredients are not important or even essential. But some things are more essential than others. Wheat bread can only be made with wheat. And while each ingredient supplies a different need, flour is the mainstay of the recipe. Paul's recipe for peace also has a key ingredient.

Scan the book of Philippians again. A good exercise might be to jot down or highlight in your Bible every positive attitude mentioned in its four chapters. You will find that throughout the letter, no fewer than a dozen of these attitudes are listed. They are peace (1:2; 4:7); thankfulness (1:3; 4:6); joy (1:4, 25; 2:2, 29; 4:1); rejoicing (1:18, 26; 2:17-18, 28; 3:1; 4:4); love (1:9, 17; 2:1-2); hope (1:20); confidence (1:25; 3:4; 4:13); encouragement (2:19; 3:4; 4:13); compassion (1:2); humility (2:3, 8); forbearance (4:5); and contentment (4:11).

References to "joy" and "rejoicing in the Lord" are found 15 times, and their repetitive use has led scholars to view them as the key word and phrase of the book. Some have called Philippians "Paul's Joy Letter."[1]

Unspeakable Joy!

"Rejoice in the Lord always. Again I will say, rejoice!" (Philippians 4:4). Paul could not have made his point any more forcefully. Having a sense of joy in our hearts is absolutely essential if we want to experience peace of mind. Joy is the flour in our bread of peace. It isn't surprising that Paul's discussion of the Spirit in Galatians 5:22 begins with love, joy and peace – three of his favorite themes. These elements of faith are so highly regarded in Scripture that they are written about in superlative terms:

- "Joy *inexpressible*" (1 Peter 1:8)
- "The love of Christ which *passes knowledge*" (Ephesians 3:19)
- "Peace ... which *surpasses all understanding*" (Philippians 4:7)

But how, when we are facing discouragement and needing peace so desperately, can we start with joy? As children we sang about these wonderful attributes. "I've got the joy, joy, joy, joy down in my heart ... I've got the love of Jesus, love of Jesus down in my heart ... I've got the peace that passes understanding down in my heart – down in my heart to stay!" But sometimes the joy manages to escape us.

Joy in Tribulation

How can a Christian be cheerful in the face of disappointment? Elton Trueblood, in *The Humor of Christ*, says it is "not because he is blind to injustice and suffering, but because he is convinced that these, in the light of the divine sovereignty, are never ultimate."[2] Romans 5:3 says we rejoice in our sufferings (RSV) because the love of God has been poured out within our hearts through the Holy Spirit. The result is peace with God (v. 1). Who cannot feel a sense of elation when reading about the love that God has for us?

But God, who is rich in mercy, because of His great love with which He loved us, even when we were dead in trespasses, made us alive together with Christ (by grace you have been saved), and raised us up together, and made us sit together in the heavenly places in Christ Jesus (Ephesians 2:4-6).

In light of the richness of our salvation, Christians should be the most joyful people on the earth – and that joy lends itself to a feeling of security.

A Time to Laugh

The Greek word for "joy" is *chara*, and it suggests a very glad feeling. It is similar in meaning to happiness, although happiness is often associated with pleasure, whereas joy is more characteristic of peace. Joy is that state of mind that allows a person to feel elated (to rejoice, *chairo*) even when circumstances are not pleasurable.

James 1:2-3 says, "[C]ount it all joy when you fall into various trials, knowing that the testing of your faith produces patience." James was saying that even when we undergo trying times, we can take comfort in knowing that our God can turn those trials into a source of blessing. This knowledge can produce a feeling of well-being and confidence.

Many people in our fun-crazed society confuse "good times" with happiness. Solomon, who did not withhold any pleasure from his heart, concluded later in his life that laughter is madness (Ecclesiastes 2:2). Keil and Delitzsch, in their commentary on Ecclesiastes, suggest that Solomon is describing the kind of laughter associated with sensual delight and a self-destruction that disregards all appropriate boundaries.[3] The "party animal" depicted so often in movies will eventually discover that this kind of fun, rather than filling life with joy, only increases an inner void. How many times have we seen this demonstrated by very public figures who experiment with every possible excess until they have spun completely out of control?

Good, clean fun, on the other hand, is healthy. In fact, Proverbs 15:15 declares that a cheerful heart has a continual feast. Elton Trueblood concluded that Jesus Himself must have had a sense of humor because so many of His parables – like the one about the man who strains out a gnat and then swallows a camel (Matthew 23:24) – have a humorous element to them.[4] And a hearty laugh really can be therapeutic. The Scriptures recommend it (Ecclesiastes 3:4).

What Happiness Isn't

The word translated "happy" in our English Bibles comes from the Greek word *makarios*, which means "blessed." It is less an emotion than a state of being. Because the word is used so loosely today, as in "happy-go-lucky" and "happy hour," some misconceptions have arisen. Among them are these:

• *Happiness is an inherent right.* Our Declaration of Independence states that all people are endowed by their Creator with certain unalienable rights, among which are life, liberty and the *pursuit* of happiness. In a free society we can make choices that we think will lead to our happiness, and as long as those choices do not infringe upon the rights of others, we can do as we please. That's a long way from saying that happiness is an entitlement or that we "deserve" to be happy. Certainly, other people are not obligated to provide everything that each of us believes we need to be happy.

• *Happiness can be bought.* Ecclesiastes 5:10 says, "He who loves money will not be satisfied with money, nor he who loves abundance with its income" (NASB). Happiness is not a product that can be purchased from the grocer's shelves. It is, instead, a rebate that comes back to you when you follow the Manufacturer's directions. Psalm 128:1-2 relates that happiness comes to those who fear the Lord and walk in His ways, adding that "[w]hen you eat the labor of your hands, You shall be happy, and it shall be well with you." It has been rightly said that true happiness can be sought, thought or caught – but never bought.

• *Happiness is derived only from pleasurable things.* Solomon realized that the heart can be glad even in times of sorrow (Ecclesiastes 7:3). Although we all feel blue at times, the child of God has hope (Romans 12:12). In delivering the "beautiful attitudes" in Matthew 5:3-10, Jesus promised that those who are persecuted for righteousness' sake are blessed because the kingdom of heaven is theirs. As we have noted, Jesus was able to get through His most trying time by looking forward to the joy that awaited Him (Hebrews 12:2).

Why Be Happy?

Sometimes it takes real effort to be upbeat. Some would ask, "Why fake what we don't feel?" There are some good reasons to try, according to the Bible.

(1) *Joy is fruit of the Spirit* (Galatians 5:22). A glum disposition indicates that the Spirit of God is not alive and well in our hearts.

(2) *A joyful disposition is healthy.* Proverbs 17:22 says, "A joyful heart is good medicine, But a broken spirit dries up the bones" (NASB). S.I. McMillen has written,

> The sincere acceptance of the principles and teach-ings of Christ with respect to the life of mental peace and joy, the life of unselfish thought and clean living, would at once wipe out more than half the difficulties, diseases and sorrows of the human race.[5]

(3) *God commands us to rejoice* (1 Thessalonians 5:16). God promised His people in the Old Testament era that if they failed to obey Him with joy and a glad heart, they would reap curses upon themselves (Deuteronomy 28:47-48). Surely, He would not expect less from those who have tasted the heavenly gift.

The Old Testament psalms encouraged worshipers to lift up their voices and express their joy. Consider these verses:

- "But let all those rejoice who put their trust in You; Let them ever shout for joy" (Psalm 5:11).

- "And my soul shall be joyful in the Lord; It shall rejoice in His salvation" (35:9).

- "Make a joyful shout to God, all the earth! Sing out the honor of His name; Make His praise glorious" (66:1-2).

- "Sing aloud to God our strength; Make a joyful shout to the God of Jacob" (81:1).

- "Oh come, let us sing to the Lord! Let us shout joyfully to the Rock of our salvation" (95:1).

- "Shout joyfully to the Lord, all the earth; Break forth in song, rejoice, and sing praises" (98:4).

- "Make a joyful shout to the Lord, all you lands! Serve the Lord with gladness; Come before His presence with singing" (100:1-2).

(4) *Finally, forcing yourself to be joyful works!* Perhaps you've heard it said, "It is easier to act your way into feeling than to feel your way into acting." It is unclear who first coined this expression, but it's true. Joy, like *agape* love, is as much a choice as it is a feeling. And the more we act on that choice, the more we are able to experience it.

Sifting Through the Lumps

A well-equipped kitchen most likely has a sifter among its utensils. We use it to add fullness to flour that has had time to settle. So often, as Christian women, we settle into a routine of family and work responsibilities. These tasks, along with church work and other duties, can cause us to neglect the joy that should be ours in Christ. When that happens, we need

> **SIFT**
>
> *verb – To pass through a sieve so as to separate the coarse from the fine particles; to break up lumps.*

to stir up our love for God and others in order to remove the lumps of doubt, discouragement, distrust, disappointment, etc., that are weighing us down.

Did you know that God has been known to discipline people by sifting them? The prophet Amos wrote how Jehovah was going to place Israel into His sieve along with neighboring nations (Amos 9:9). He intended to sift them as the women in ancient times sifted their grain: by tossing it into the air. The good kernels would fall through the sieve to the ground, while the worthless chaff would be blown away (Psalm 1:4). Have you ever felt that *your* life is being turned upside down? Perhaps during these times, God is allowing you to be sifted so you might remember what is truly important in life.

Do my priorities need to be rearranged? Has my joy become heavy? God can help. "Ask, and you will receive, that your joy may be full" (John 16:24).

Questions to Chew On
1. Why has Philippians been called "Paul's Joy Letter?"

2. What superlative qualities do the Scriptures ascribe to love, joy and peace?

3. How can a Christian be cheerful in the face of discouragement?

4. What was the attitude of Christ Jesus toward the sacrifice He made on our behalf (Hebrews 12:2)?

5. How is the Bible's definition of happiness different from current usage?

6. What did Solomon say about laughter? Why?

7. What does Proverbs 15:15 say about a cheerful heart?

8. Discuss some misconceptions about happiness.

9. Give three reasons why we should be joyful.

10. Read Ecclesiastes 7:3-4. Discuss what these verses might mean.

FOOD for THOUGHT

"All the days of the afflicted are evil, But he who is of a merry heart has a continual feast" (Proverbs 15:15).

TAKE OUT

He who continually searches for happiness will never find it. Happiness is made, not found.

PRAYER *List*

_____

_____

_____

_____

_____

_____

_____

_____

_____

_____

_____

_____

_____

_____

_____

_____

 # SWEETENERS

God must have created Adam with a sweet tooth because people have always loved sweets and have found a variety of ways to satisfy their cravings.

In Old Testament days fruits and honey served as the primary source of sweetening. Figs were a delicacy when eaten young and green, but most were dried into fig cakes (1 Samuel 25:18; 1 Chronicles 12:40). Raisins and dates also were eaten this way. Many homes had cultivated vines and fig trees growing outside that provided fruit for eating and cooking (1 Kings 4:25).

Israelite women boiled down some of their fruits into syrup which they used not only for cooking but also for drinking when mixed with water. Wild honey was especially prized for its sweetness and was used in baking (Genesis 43:11; 1 Kings 14:3).

Sally Lunn Bread

The recipe for Sally Lunn Bread is among those recipes that have been around so long that they were originally called "receipts." Some think the recipe originated in Bath, England, and was brought to the colonies where it appeared in many early American cookbooks. Many variations exist, some made with yeast and some with baking powder. The amount of sugar varies according to taste.

Ingredients

¾ cup milk
½ cup melted shortening
3¼ cups plain flour
½ teaspoon salt
¾ cup sugar
4 tablespoons warm water
1 (¼ ounce) package active dry yeast
1 egg
Butter

Directions

Grease a baking sheet. Heat the milk and shortening to luke-warm, and set aside. Mix flour, salt and sugar in a bowl. Add the 4 tablespoons of warm water to the yeast in a separate bowl. Add the warm milk mixture to the flour mixture. Add the egg and yeast mixture. Beat the mixture until it leaves the sides of the bowl. Cover and let rise in a warm place until double in size, about 90 minutes. Knead down in size, and shape into a round loaf. Place on baking sheet and allow dough to rise again to half as big, about 45 minutes. Bake at 300 degrees for approximately 45 minutes. After the first 30 minutes, baste the top with butter and again after it has finished baking. Yield: one 2-pound loaf.

CHAPTER 6

A SPOONFUL OF SWEETNESS

How sweet, how heavenly, is the sight,
When those that love the Lord
In one another's peace delight
And so fulfill His Word!
　　　　　－ Joseph Swain, 1792 [1]

The words of this beautiful hymn may sound familiar. Some of us grew up in congregations where this song was sung often, and the sweet fellowship it describes figured significantly into the persons we have become. The hymn is reminiscent of Psalm 133, a song that the priests and Levites probably sang on their way to the temple. "Behold, how good and how pleasant it is For brethren to dwell together in unity!" (v. 1).

Many of my childhood recollections are wrapped around the church – little vignettes of the senses that have become precious memories: the taste of grape juice from pastel-colored cups at vacation Bible school; the smell of brand-new crayons and workbooks at Sunday school promotion; dinner on the grounds with fried chicken and potato salad; open windows and funeral-home fans; the sounds of congregational singing under a tent; and the visual wonder of Bible lessons told on a flannelgraph board.

Sowers of Discord

But those sweet experiences were marred occasionally by "church problems" here and there. Some involved doctrinal disagreements, while others occurred because of power struggles or careless words of criticism. Sometimes problems disrupted fellowship between loving people who had worshiped together for years. Is it any wonder that the Scriptures say God hates the sowing of discord among brethren (Proverbs 6:16-19)?

Jude described certain people in the first-century church who crept in, unnoticed, to destroy the unity of the brethren. They did it by rejecting authority, finding fault, grumbling and speaking arrogantly. They also corrupted the purity of the church by condoning and even promoting activities that were sensual and had no place among Christians.

The Living Bible paraphrases Jude 16 this way: "These men are constant gripers, never satisfied, doing whatever evil they feel like; they are loud-mouthed 'show-offs'; and when they show respect for others, it is only to get something from them in return." Jude said they were "hidden reefs" in the love feasts of the church (Jude 12 NASB). The idea is that these individuals were like dangerous rocks upon which an unsuspecting vessel might become shipwrecked. The damage they caused could be considerable.

A Warning

It is unclear from the text exactly what problems were brewing in the church at Philippi. Chapter 3 begins with a warning about some people whom Paul classified as "dogs" (Philippians 3:2). This may be a reference to their low character as well as their vicious and sneaky nature. They entered the church quietly but attacked when they did not get what they wanted. Paul told the Philippians to be wary of such people. He appealed to the church to stand firm in one spirit, "with one mind striving together for the faith of the gospel" (Philippians 1:27). He told them,

Therefore if there is any encouragement in Christ, if there is any consolation of love, if there is any fellowship of the Spirit, if any affection and compassion, make my joy complete by being of the same mind, maintaining the same love, united in spirit, intent on one purpose. Do nothing from selfishness or empty conceit, but with humility of mind regard one another as more important than yourselves; do not merely look out for your own personal interests, but also for the interests of others (Philippians 2:1-4 NASB).

Paul, like Jude, warned about those who initiate unrest by grumbling and complaining. He added:

Do all things without complaining and disputing, that you may become blameless and harmless, children of God without fault in the midst of a crooked and perverse generation, among whom you shine as lights in the world (Philippians 2:14-15).

A Plea for Harmony

Disunity apparently was brewing at Philippi. Paul mentioned the two women involved by name and appealed for help in getting these sisters to work out their differences. They were good women, fellow workers in the gospel; but something had created such a rift between them that the whole church was being affected (Philippians 4:2-3).

In light of the discouragement that a "church fuss" always causes, Paul urged the congregation to practice forbearance with each other. He wrote, "Let your forbearance be known unto all men. The Lord is at hand" (Philippians 4:5 ASV).

Some in the early church thought Christ's return was eminent, so Paul may have been advising them to be ready. It is also possible he was emphasizing that the Lord was well aware of what was going on and that He expected certain things of them if they were going to wear His name.

One Fold

Jesus compared the church to a sheepfold. The word "fold" in this context means an enclosed place and is closely related to an Old English word that means "to draw together." The purpose of the fold was to keep the sheep together, thus providing protection for them. Jesus told his Jewish disciples that He must bring other sheep into His fold. By

---

FOLD

noun – enclosed place
verb – to blend an ingredi-
ent into a mixture, using
gentle, cutting strokes.

---

that He meant the Gentiles, and He added, "and there shall be one fold, and one shepherd" (John 10:16 KJV). It was not always easy for both groups in the first century to worship together. It required real effort to live in harmony during that era, just as it sometimes does today when people have different opinions about how things should be done.

Forbearance

The term "forbearance" in Philippians 4:5 is translated "moderation" in the King James Version. The New King James Version and New International Version translate the word as "gentleness." The New American Standard Bible says, "gentle spirit"; and the English Standard Version translates it as "reasonableness." The Greek word used is *epieikes*, an adjective that means "forbearing." Matthew Arnold calls this attitude "sweet reasonableness." [2]

Forbearance is an expression of gentleness that does not fly off the handle easily or make a mountain out of every molehill. Vine says "it expresses that considerateness that looks humanely and reasonably at the facts of a case." [3] It is patient rather than contentious. Because we all offend in many ways, we need the understanding of others (James 3:2 KJV). That means we need to cut them some slack as well. Too often personal disagreements lead to cliques that shut some individuals out of the fellowship. Edwin Markham's famous poem "Outwitted" reminds us that, when possible, love seeks to bring others into our fold rather than shut them out:

> He drew a circle that shut me out –
> Heretic, rebel, a thing to flout.
> But Love and I had the wit to win:
> We drew a circle that took him in.[4]

Gentleness

I have a friend who says his goal in life is to become a sweet old man. Gentleness is a manly quality associated with Christ (Matthew 21:5 NASB). It is closely related to meekness, although neither English word really conveys the strength of character implied in these passages where *epeikes* ("gentle") is used:

- Elders must not be "given to wine, not violent, not greedy for money, but gentle, not quarrelsome, not covetous" (1 Timothy 3:3).

- The brethren, also, must "speak evil of no one ... be peaceable, gentle, showing all humility to all men" (Titus 3:2).

- The wisdom from above is "first pure, then peaceable, gentle, willing to yield, full of mercy and good fruits, without partiality and without hypocrisy" (James 3:17).

Problems in the church have to be dealt with firmly but reasonably. Elders often must rule with an "iron hand in a velvet glove," a phrase attributed to Napoleon in describing a good ruler.[5]

Patience

Being sweet and reasonable is difficult when we are stressed and under pressure. How easily we can relate to Martha, whose friendship with Jesus is recorded in Luke 10:38-42. What an energetic lady she was! It is not hard to visualize her fussing over a visit that He made to her home. There was much to do, and she was distracted by all the preparations – so much that she forgot the most important thing: that Jesus was present!

When Martha complained to Him that her sister was sitting and listening rather than helping, Jesus gave her a gentle reprimand

– probably one she never forgot: "Martha, Martha, you are worried and bothered about so many things; but only a few things are necessary, for Mary has chosen the good part, which shall not be taken away from her" (Luke 10:41-42 NASB).

Martha was probably a very kind and generous person. That she is remembered most often for this one incident is unfortunate. Whenever we react impatiently toward a co-worker on the job, or complain irritably to a busy salesclerk, or speak discourteously to the person who comes to our door with a religious tract in hand – we may be making a lasting negative impression. How unfortunate to be remembered for a moment of rudeness.

Sweet Reasonableness

John earned the name "The Apostle of Love." It was said that in his old age, he went about admonishing Christians to love one another. His writings suggest that he, too, became a sweet old man, even though he remained passionate about defending the truth.

His temperament had not always been so gentle, however. Luke recorded an incident when John and his brother James were rebuked by the Lord for an unreasonable request. It happened as Jesus and the disciples were passing through Samaria and were refused hospitality by the people of one village. The brothers were so offended that they wanted to call down fire from heaven to consume the townspeople. But these "Sons of Thunder" (Mark 3:17) were overreacting. Jesus said to them, "You do not know what manner of spirit you are of. For the Son of Man did not come to destroy men's lives but to save them" (Luke 9:55-56).

A Little Sweetness

My Grandmother Jackson used to put a teaspoon of sugar into almost everything she cooked. That touch of sugar helped to satisfy the appetites of those living on the farm who craved something sweet. Someone has said, "Be kind. Every person you meet is fighting some difficult battle." If that be true, it can't hurt to fold a spoonful of sweetness into all our dealings with other people. They may need it more than we know.

Questions to Chew On

1. Do you have sweet memories of happy times in the church? What are they?

2. Why does God hate discord among brethren?

3. What are some meanings for the word "forbearance"?

4. Why should we be patient with people who are disagreeable?

5. The church is described as a "fold." What does this suggest about the way we should treat one another?

6. Why is gentleness an important qualification for elders in the church?

7. Discuss the incident at the home of Mary and Martha. Are you a Mary or a Martha, or do you relate to both?

8. What is the lesson learned from Luke 10:41-42?

9. Discuss the statement, "Every person you meet is fighting some difficult battle." Do you believe that is true?

10. Can one learn to be sweet and gentle if that is not her typical disposition? Give examples.

FOOD *for* THOUGHT

"Who among you is wise and under-standing? Let him show by his good behavior his deeds in the gentleness of wisdom" (James 3:13 NASB).

TAKE OUT

Patience is often bitter, but its fruit is sweet.

PRAYER *List*

A GOOD EGG

The age-old question, "Which came first, the chicken or the egg?" is answered in Genesis 1:21-23, where we learn that on the fifth day of creation, God made every winged fowl with the ability to reproduce. Eggs likely became a part of the human diet early on.

The Israelites probably included eggs from pigeons, ducks, geese, game birds and ostriches in their diets. Job ate them. And like many of us, he found the egg white to be tasteless without salt (Job 6:6). Proverbs 30:31 mentions the rooster (NASB), and we know for sure that chickens were common throughout Palestine in New Testament days.

Jesus taught that our heavenly Father is caring and is eager to meet our needs when we ask. He said, if a son "asks for an egg, will [any father] offer him a scorpion?" (Luke 11:11-12). He later used the touching illustration of a mother hen gathering up her chicks to describe how badly He had often longed to draw the Jewish people to Him (Matthew 23:37).

Eggs are high in nutritional value – an excellent source of protein. They also are emulsifiers, meaning they add volume and disperse the ingredients in a mixture, greatly enhancing the taste and quality. The more eggs you add, the richer the flavor and texture. Some preparations, such as angel food cake, call for the whites only. Others (custards, for example) call only for the yolk. But as a rule, the whole egg is blended in.

Think of prayer as the egg in your recipe. A healthy blending of supplication and thanksgiving will add to the fullness of life. The more we add, the richer life becomes.

Egg Bread

Ingredients

2 (2½ ounce) packages active dry yeast
⅔ cup warm water (110 degrees)
6 egg yolks
3 eggs at room temperature
½ cup vegetable oil
¼ cup white sugar
1 teaspoon salt
5 cups all-purpose flour
1 egg
A pinch of salt

Directions

In a large bowl, dissolve yeast in warm water. Stir in the yolks, 3 eggs, oil, sugar and salt. Add about 3½ cups of flour to make a sticky dough.

Turn the dough out onto a lightly floured surface. Knead with remaining flour until smooth and elastic, about 7 minutes. Place in a well-oiled bowl, turning to oil the entire surface of the dough. Cover with a damp cloth, and place in a warm spot until double in size, about 90 minutes.

Punch down the dough, and divide it into 3 pieces. Roll each piece into a rope about 12 inches long. Braid the three strands together, sealing the ends. Place the bread on a greased cookie sheet. Beat the one remaining egg with a pinch of salt; brush onto bread. Let the bread rise until doubled, about 45 minutes. Preheat the oven to 375 degrees. Brush the bread with the egg wash again. Bake at 375 degrees for 40 minutes or until golden. Cool on a wire rack. Yield: 1 braided loaf.

CHAPTER 7

A BINDING OF PRAYER

P aul was a praying man. The brethren at Philippi knew that. They could remember a time when Paul and Silas had been beaten and put into stocks in the inner prison of their city. As the two were praying and singing around midnight, an earthquake rocked the prison and freed them from their bonds. By choosing to remain in their cell rather than flee, Paul gained an opportunity to preach the gospel to a jailer and his family. The result was that the man and his entire household were baptized into Christ the same night (Acts 16:22-34).

Whenever Paul talked about prayer, he knew from experience the power that it can unleash. The incident at Philippi was one of many examples of answered prayer in his life. Paul's letter to the Philippians reveals that Paul prayed regularly and believed in its effectiveness.

- "I thank my God upon every remembrance of you, always in every prayer of mine making request for you all with joy, for your fellowship in the gospel from the first day until now" (Philippians 1:3-5).

- "And this I pray, that your love may abound still more and more in knowledge and all discernment" (v. 9).

- "For I know that this will turn out for my deliverance through your prayer and the supply of the Spirit of Jesus Christ" (v. 19).

- "Be anxious for nothing, but in everything by prayer and supplication, with thanksgiving, let your requests be made known to God" (4:6).

God's Promise

One of the great promises of Scripture is that God wants people to come to Him with their needs. Peter says that the Lord's eyes are upon the righteous, and His ears are open to their prayers (1 Peter 3:12). Here Peter is quoting from Psalm 34:15-16, in which the psalmist uses an anthropomorphism – a reference to God using human terminology. Notice, however, that God's promise to acknowledge our prayers is conditional:

> When I shut up heaven and there is no rain, or command the locusts to devour the land, or send pestilence among My people, if My people who are called by My name will humble themselves, and pray and seek My face, and turn from their wicked ways, then I will hear from heaven, and will forgive their sin and heal their land (2 Chronicles 7:13-14).

> For this cause everyone who is godly shall pray to You In a time when You may be found … (Psalm 32:6).

> The righteous cry out, and the Lord hears, And delivers them out of all their troubles (Psalm 34:17).

Prayer Binds Us to God

Prayer, in some ways, is like the egg in our bread recipe. It serves many purposes. Eggs serve as thickening agents and add richness to sauces, custards and puddings; and they bind all the other ingredients together. They also serve to leaven the mixture, causing it to rise. God has commanded us to pray because prayer has many benefits. It takes us into the presence of Jehovah, where there is "fullness of joy" (Psalm 16:11).

BIND

verb – to hold ingredients together.

It can serve to hold us together when we don't know where to turn, and in the process it lightens our load and lifts our spirits.

Jesus and Prayer

Jesus' prayer life was not confined to a few short moments each day. We can readily see evidence of this in these instances recorded in the gospel accounts:

- He prayed following His baptism (Luke 3:21).
- He prayed for His enemies (Matthew 5:44).
- He rose to pray very early in the morning after a long day at Capernaum (Mark 1:35).
- He gave thanks before eating (Matthew 14:19; 26:26-27).
- He prayed throughout the night after feeding the 5,000 (Matthew 14:23).
- He prayed for the little children who were brought to Him (Matthew 19:13).
- He often withdrew into the wilderness to pray (Luke 5:16).
- He spent an entire night in prayer before appointing the twelve (Luke 6:12).
- He was praying when He was transfigured (Luke 9:28-29).
- He prayed publicly before raising Lazarus from the dead (John 11:41).
- He prayed alone in Gethsemane before His betrayal (Matthew 26:36).
- He prayed from the cross (Luke 23:34).

The Lord prayed at all times of the day or night, sometimes privately and sometimes in the presence of others. He prayed kneeling (Luke 22:41) and sometimes prostrate before God (Matthew 26:39). It was customary for the Pharisees to stand when they prayed (Matthew 6:5; Mark 11:25; Luke 18:11-13). Whether Jesus ever adopted that posture, we don't know. But sometimes He prayed looking up to heaven (Matthew 14:19; Luke 9:16). He prayed as He hung from the cross, demonstrating that God notes the disposition of our hearts more than our body posture.

Teach Us to Pray

After one season of prayer, Jesus' disciples came to Him with a request. "Lord, teach us to pray, as John also taught his disciples" (Luke 11:1). Jesus then gave them a model prayer that is surprisingly brief. Because God knows our needs before we ask, His words on this occasion were few and simple. Jesus prayed,

Our Father in heaven, Hallowed be Your name. Your kingdom come. Your will be done On earth as it is in heaven. Give us this day our daily bread. And forgive us our debts, As we forgive our debtors. And do not lead us into temptation, But deliver us from the evil one. For Yours is the kingdom and the power and the glory forever. Amen (Matthew 6:9-13).

This model prayer, often called "The Lord's Prayer," included praise and thanksgiving along with petition. It teaches us that we should blend these same elements into our personal prayers. Jesus addressed the Father with praise and reverence. He began one prayer by saying, "I praise You, Father, Lord of heaven and earth" (Luke 10:21). In this, He was following a pattern common in the psalms: "Give unto the

BLEND

verb – to mix thoroughly so that the individual parts are merged together.

Lord the glory due to His name" (Psalm 29:2).

At other times Jesus began with praise and thanksgiving: "I thank You, Father, Lord of heaven and earth" (Matthew 11:25). This is also a pattern in the psalms:

- "It is good to give thanks to the Lord, And to sing praises to Your name, O Most High" (Psalm 92:1).

- "Enter into His gates with thanksgiving, And into His courts with praise. Be thankful to Him, and bless His name" (100:4).

Jesus emphasized that because God is our Father, we also can ask for whatever we need. In the model prayer He gave these examples:

• *He prayed that the kingdom might be established according to God's divine plan.* This prayer was later fulfilled when the church was established on the Day of Pentecost (Acts 2). Jesus has purchased the church with His blood (Acts 20:28), and all those purchased by His blood make up the kingdom (Revelation 1:4-5; 5:9-10). Paul could assure the Colossians that God had delivered them (past tense) out of darkness and had conveyed them into the kingdom of His Son, where there is redemption through His blood (Colossians 1:13-14; Revelation 1:5-6). Because the kingdom has already been established, it would be inappropriate for Christians today to pray that the kingdom might come in the future, but it would not be wrong to ask that it continue to spread to people who have never heard of it.

• *He prayed for the Father's will to be done on earth as it is in heaven.* This petition reveals that Jesus was not self-willed. Submitting to His Father required tremendous strength and determination on His part (Philippians 2:8). We should trust God enough that we are willing to accept His judgment in answering our requests, and we need to express this often.

• *He taught that we should ask God for our daily needs.* Jesus prayed, "Give us this day our daily bread" (Matthew 6:11). This reminds us that we are not self-sufficient. The children of Israel were given manna in the wilderness on a daily basis so they might learn that "man shall not live by bread alone; but man lives by every word that proceeds from the mouth of the Lord" (Deuteronomy 8:3). Because they had to gather their food every morning but the Sabbath, they were constantly being reminded that Jehovah would care for them as long as they followed His commands.

Jesus taught that God hasn't just *agreed* to supply our needs; He *wants* to do it. What a comforting yet humbling thought. So He urged the disciples,

> Ask, and it will be given to you; seek, and you will find; knock, and it will be opened to you. For everyone who asks receives, and he who seeks finds, and to him who knocks it will be opened. Or what man is there among you who, if his son asks for bread, will give him a stone? Or if he asks for a fish, will he give him a serpent? If you then, being evil, know how to give good gifts to your children, how much more will your Father who is in heaven give good things to those who ask Him! (Matthew 7:7-11).

Sometimes we lack what we need because we have never humbled ourselves to ask God for it. Also, wants and needs are not always the same. When we ask like a child begging sweets from the cookie jar, God sometimes says no (James 4:2-3). Most of us can think of a time when God did not answer a prayer as we had hoped. And sometimes in hindsight, we are very thankful.

• *He taught that we should seek God's forgiveness.* Jesus instructed the disciples to pray, "[F]orgive us our debts, As we forgive our debtors" (Matthew 6:12). Repeatedly, He warned that our personal forgiveness depends upon the grace we are willing to extend to others. The familiar parable of the unforgiving servant reinforces this fact (Matthew 18:21-35).

Jesus' model prayer consists of only five verses in our New Testament. Not every thought we send to God will include each of these elements. An evening sunset may evoke a heartfelt, "Thank you, Lord! You are so great and powerful!" Disturbing news may call for a hurried, "O Lord, help!" But each of us needs times of regular thoughtful prayer in which our requests are prefaced with praise and words of thanksgiving.

A Note of Caution

It is good to remember that one part of the egg has no nutritional value, and if it slips into the mix, it needs to be removed. Break the shell and discard it; otherwise, it may interfere with the taste or texture of the egg. (It may also keep egg whites from forming a meringue.) Self-righteousness, like that shell, has no place in our prayer life and will keep our petitions from being effective. Jesus brought this lesson home with a story about two men who went to the temple to pray. One left justified; the other did not (Luke 18:9-14). Jesus told the parable to warn about the danger of trusting in our own personal righteousness while we look down upon others. Often it is our pride rather than God's willingness to bless that prevents our prayers from being answered.

Questions to Chew On

1. Name some nutritional properties of eggs. How might they symbolize the prayer in our recipe?

2. Describe the incident in Acts 16:22-34 where prayer was answered for Paul and Silas.

3. What is an anthropomorphism? What does Scripture say about God's eyes and ears in Psalm 34? What can we infer from this?

4. What did Psalm 95:6 invite worshipers to do? Did Jesus often pray this way? Can we conclude that this is the only acceptable way to pray?

5. How did the model prayer begin that Jesus prayed with His disciples (Matthew 6:9-13)?

6. Name four things Jesus taught the disciples to pray for.

7. Should we pray for God's kingdom to come in some future sense? Why or why not?

8. Why did Jesus pray, "Give us this day our daily bread"?

9. Discuss reasons why some of our prayers might not be answered as we hoped they would.

10. Upon what does God's forgiveness hinge?

FOOD *for* THOUGHT

"The prayer of a righteous person is powerful and effective" (James 5:16 NIV).

TAKE OUT

If you would have God hear you when you pray,
you must hear Him when He speaks.

PRAYER *List*

_____

_____

_____

_____

_____

_____

_____

_____

_____

_____

_____

_____

_____

_____

_____

_____

FATS AND OILS

The patriarchs considered the fat of an animal to be the best part, and from earliest times the fat was devoted to God. Genesis 4:4 says that Abel brought the firstborn of his flock and "of their fat" as his offering. Later, under the Law of Moses, the fat of the animal being sacrificed belonged to God. The priest burned it on the altar as a "sweet aroma" to Him (Leviticus 3:16). The "fat" in Scripture always signifies the best part (Genesis 45:18).

Our grandmothers often used animal fat – mostly lard – in their cooking, but Israelite women relied on olive oil. Olives, plentiful in Palestine, served many purposes. The oil fueled their lamps and served as ointment for their bodies, but mostly it was used in cooking.

Butter was also a source of fat in their diets. Butter is thought to have been made from soured milk poured into a goatskin bag and shaken until the oily "butter" separated. This was probably the kind of butter Abraham and Sarah served their guests in Genesis 18:8. The Hebrew word is sometimes translated as cream, curds or cheese.

Challah

Today "challah" refers to the bread eaten by many Jewish people on the Sabbath and holidays. Originally, "challah" referred to the small piece of dough that was set aside for the priest when making bread (Numbers 15:20). Today Jewish women bless, separate and burn a small piece of dough when making this bread in remembrance of the portion given to God in ancient times through the temple priests.

Ingredients
1 teaspoon sugar
½ cup warm water
1 package yeast
½ cup oil
½ cup warm water
¼ cup sugar
2 teaspoons salt
2 eggs
3½ to 4 cups all-purpose flour
1 egg yolk beaten with 1 teaspoon water
Poppy and/or sesame seeds

Directions
Dissolve sugar in ½ cup warm water in large mixing bowl that has first been rinsed with hot water. Sprinkle yeast on top, and let stand for 10 minutes. Stir to dissolve. Combine with oil, ½ cup warm water, sugar, salt, eggs and half of the flour. Beat well. Stir in remaining flour. Dough should be sticky. Cover dough, and let rest for 10 minutes. Turn out onto a floured board and knead for 10 minutes, adding flour as needed. Round up in a greased bowl. Cover and let rise in a warm place until double in bulk, about 1½ to 2 hours. Punch down, cover and let rise again until double, about 45 minutes. Divide dough into 3 equal parts. Shape into long strands. Place on a lightly greased baking sheet, and braid loosely. Fasten ends securely, using dab of water to help make the seal, if necessary. Cover with a damp cloth, and let rise until doubled in size. Brush top and sides with beaten egg yolk mixture, and sprinkle generously with seeds. Bake at 400 degrees for 30 minutes or until golden brown. Yield: 1 braided loaf.

CHAPTER 8

GIVE GOD THE FAT

Maybe you have gone to the refrigerator on occasion and removed a plate of food several days old. If the leftovers passed the "sniff test," you may have eaten them, only to find your stomach rumbling and your head aching several hours later. Chances are, you had contracted food poisoning.

According to the Centers for Disease Control, millions of people suffer from food poisoning every year, and some of them end up in the hospital. In rare cases these kinds of infections can even cause death. Altogether more than 250 different food-borne diseases exist, most caused by bacteria, viruses and parasites. The toxins are everywhere, and they tend to multiply once the food is eaten. To avoid getting sick, these safety guidelines are recommended:

- Practice cleanliness – handle food with care.
- Separate foods – avoid cross-contamination.
- Store foods at proper temperatures – avoid lukewarm foods.
- Be thorough in cooking.
- Don't sample what you are unsure about eating.[1]

The best-known rule of all is, "If in doubt, throw it out!" These guidelines have a spiritual application as well because our souls are very much in danger of being poisoned by corruption that is everywhere in this world (Ephesians 4:22). It has the potential to make us spiritually sick and can even result in spiritual death.

The Law of Moses

The Law of Moses contained a number of regulations that were ceremonial and religious in nature but also served to promote good health. The Israelites quarantined those who were diseased (Leviticus 13:46). They took precautions when they touched the carcass of any animal that was unclean, and they could not eat the meat of these unclean animals (11:8, 28). Pork, which we know carries bacteria unless properly cooked, was among those forbidden meats. They also practiced sanitation in disposing of human waste (Deuteronomy 23:12-13).

When in Doubt

Whatever the mind feeds upon directly impacts the soul's well-being. To avoid becoming "sin-sick," we can apply the same guidelines mentioned earlier.

• *Practice cleanliness.* "Cleanliness is next to godliness" is an axiom not found in the Bible, but the principle is there. The Levite priests had to wash themselves in the laver before they could enter the Holy Place of the temple. This ceremonial cleansing was a reminder that nothing unclean could enter into God's presence (Exodus 30:18-20). In the Christian dispensation, believers are cleansed by the blood of Christ in the waters of baptism before entering the house of God, which is the church. Paul said we are thus able to draw near to God "with a true heart in full assurance of faith, having our hearts sprinkled [clean] from an evil conscience and our bodies washed with pure water" (Hebrews 10:22). This process, called sanctification, involves "the washing of water by the word" (Ephesians 5:26), and it separates the Christian from the unclean world in which she lives. The word "sanctified" means "set apart."

• *Avoid cross-contamination.* Scripture warns us repeatedly about the dangers of contamination. The Levites were separated from the other Israelite tribes because they had been called by God for a specific purpose (Numbers 8:14). Christians today make up God's holy priesthood (1 Peter 2:5).

When the Israelites returned from captivity, they were told to separate themselves from foreigners who would lead them away from God (Ezra 10:11). Paul repeated the principle in 2 Corinthians 6:14-17, telling the church that they must avoid entanglements with unbelievers and adding, "Come out from among them And be separate." The Greek, *ekklesia*, from which the word "church" is derived, literally means "the called out." The church is not called to a "holier-than-thou" attitude, but is called to live above the evil influences so prevalent in the world (1 Corinthians 5:9-11).

• *Keep it hot or cold.* The rule for food is to keep hot things hot and cold things cold. Keeping certain foods at room temperature allows bacteria to grow. Living with one foot in the church and the other in the world is as illogical as trying to keep food hot and cold at the same time. The result is lukewarmness, and sin breeds in a lukewarm heart. Jesus cannot stomach those who contaminate His body, and He says that He will vomit them out of His mouth (Revelation 3:15-16).

• *Be thorough in preparation.* Certain foods require thorough heating to kill bacteria. Failing to cook them for the specified time will allow the toxins to reproduce even more rapidly. The Christian who makes only a half-hearted attempt to serve Christ becomes an easy target for temptation (James 4:7). It takes real ardor – a sincere commitment – to carry us on to maturity (1:4).

• *Don't sample what you are unsure about.* Eve wrestled with whether she should sample the fruit that was so appealing and seemed to be good for food. When she yielded to the temptation to try it, she found it to be the taste of death (Genesis 3:6). When we engage in any activity we are unsure about, we violate our conscience, and that becomes sin (Romans 14:23). "Better safe than sorry" is good advice.

Think on These Things

None of us would deliberately ingest food that is spoiled. We demand high standards from eating establishments. Rather than risk contamination, we will err on the side of caution when determining what is safe. Why is it, then, that so many people willingly fill their minds with garbage? Philippians 4:8 cautions us to let our minds dwell upon the wholesome things in life because a diet of good thoughts is healthy. Specifically, Paul enumerated several kinds of things upon which we should feed.

> Finally, brethren, whatever is true, whatever is honorable, whatever is right, whatever is pure, whatever is lovely, whatever is of good repute, if there is any excellence and if anything worthy of praise, dwell on these things" (Philippians 4:8 NASB).

It's a wise woman who wills her mind to become steeped in these good things:

(1) **Whatever is true.** Aristotle once said, "Liars when they speak the truth are not believed." Maybe this is one reason why Proverbs 19:22 advises that it is better to be a poor person than a liar. The woman who constantly embellishes the truth has no credibility. Sooner or later liars get caught (v. 5). Tell the truth, and you won't have to worry about forgetting what you have said.

STEEP

verb – to immerse or saturate; to cause one substance to be absorbed into another so as to extract its essence.

Most important, Proverbs 6:16-19 teaches that a "lying tongue" and "a false witness who speaks lies" are both an abomination to God.

Ralph Waldo Emerson wrote that "God offers to every mind its choice between truth and repose. Take which you please; you can never have both."[2] He implies that telling the truth causes problems. Many people seem to have that philosophy. People are often willing to excuse dishonesty in themselves, although they expect truthfulness in others.

We are living in the Era of Postmodernism where ideas about right and wrong seem to be changing quickly. A new "science," sometimes called evolutionary psychology, claims that our values have simply evolved over time. Proponents of situation ethics teach that there are no absolute values. So, when as children we sang in Bible class, "Stand up straight and *always* tell the truth," we were voicing an old-fashioned idea. Many consider lying to be acceptable if it results in a desired end. But Proverbs 21:6 says, "Getting treasures by a lying tongue Is a fleeting fantasy of those who seek death." The path of deceit leads down the road to regret.

(2) *Whatever is honorable.* The word "honorable" in Greek (*semnos*) carries with it a sense of dignity. In the Philippians passage, Vine says "it points to seriousness of purpose and to self-respect in conduct."[3] Honor was a characteristic of the virtuous woman in Proverbs 31, of whom it was said that strength and honor were her clothing (v. 25). This woman was hard-working, benevolent, kind and reverent. Both in her dress and in her demeanor, she demanded respect. These attributes caused her to be praised by all who knew her; and this, in turn, gave her an inner confidence. The writer said she was able to rejoice at the future (v. 25). Modesty and respectful behavior are among those traits God deems precious in women (1 Peter 3:4). These qualities tend to build the positive self-esteem that is so essential to peace of mind.

(3) *Whatever is pure.* When it comes to cooking, we know that pure vanilla extract beats the imitation variety any day. We like our olive oil to be virgin. Some are convinced that bottled water is freer from impurities than water from the tap. Many will eat only kosher foods that are prepared according to traditional laws of cleanliness. We want whatever we ingest to be as unadulterated as possible.

When Jesus' disciples were challenged by the Pharisees for eating with unwashed hands, Jesus countered by saying they were more in danger of being defiled by the impurity in their hearts than by whatever might be on their hands (Matthew 15:1-20).

He spoke about the uncleanness that comes from evil thoughts, murders, adulteries, fornications, thefts, false witness and slander. Those contaminants were common in Jesus' day, and they have not been eradicated in ours.

We may be more like the Pharisees than we think. Grandma used lye soap for washing; today we have antibacterial cleaners that are supposed to kill every germ in the kitchen. Meanwhile, though, many of our homes are being inundated with a steady stream of filth that enters daily through the television, Internet and other kinds of media to which we subscribe.

Researchers tell us that the typical teenager spends nearly twice the hours in front of the television as in the classroom.[4] Excessive TV watching has been linked to violence, addictive behavior, obesity, premarital sex, profanity and disrespect for parents according to the Parents Television Council.[5] Pornography is now one of the fastest-growing addictions in the country, affecting both men and women.[6]

None of us is immune to the power of impure thoughts, as David discovered in such a tragic way. In Psalm 51 he pleaded for God's forgiveness, asking that God create within him "a clean heart" (v. 10). Thoughts and images that he could not remove without God's help had taken root in his heart. Although David found forgiveness, the consequences of unrestrained passion affected his life forever.

(4) *Whatever is lovely.* Genesis 1 states repeatedly that everything God made is good. Solomon reiterated that everything God created serves an appropriate purpose, adding that He has entrusted mankind with the job of studying His wonderful universe. He wrote, "I have seen the God-given task with which the sons of men are to be occupied. He has made everything beautiful in its time. Also He has put eternity in their hearts, except that no one can find out the work that God does from beginning to end" (Ecclesiastes 3:1-11).

Often our days are filled with so many urgent matters that we neglect to stop and think about the valuable lessons we could be learning through God's creation. Would we like to know God better? Paul wrote that "His invisible attributes are clearly seen" in the things He made (Romans 1:20). It's important, then, that we take some time to really pay attention to the physical world in which we live.

In his 1952 book, *The Power of Positive Thinking*, Norman Vincent Peale wrote about the great benefits of emptying the mind twice each day of all negative thoughts and filling it with creative and healthy thoughts from Scripture. He advocated devoting 15 minutes daily to absolute silence. [7] In Psalm 46:10, God speaks through the psalmist to say, "Be still, and know that I am God."

Do you remember when evenings in the summer were spent sitting on the porch, listening to the tree frogs and whippoorwills and watching lightning bugs light up the dusk? More often, evenings now find us "glued to the tube." It's a pity we have gotten away from quiet moments spent in reverie at the end of each day. Periods of solitude like this do a great deal to ease the stresses of everyday life.

(5) *Whatever is of good repute.* This is rendered in various translations as "whatever is kindly spoken" (ML); "whatever is gracious" (RS); or "praiseworthy" (PME). Remember the little song we learned as children, "If you can't say something nice – shhh, say nothing"? Proverbs 18:8 says that the words of a whisperer are like "dainty morsels" (NASB) that go down into the body.

Some people do seem to "feed" on rumors. Paul wrote about women who go from house to house as "gossips and busybodies, talking about things not proper to mention" (1 Timothy 5:13 NASB). The tongue, James said, is a fire that can cause great destruction (James 3:5). It has the power to ruin friendships (Proverbs 16:28). The warning is, "[She] who goes about as a slanderer reveals secrets, Therefore do not associate with a gossip" (20:19 NASB). Many a church rift has resulted from idle gossip, and God hates the sowing of "discord among brethren" (6:19).

(6) *Whatever is excellent and praiseworthy.* One of my favorite poems is "My Symphony" by W.H. Channing. [8] The poem illustrates the often-heard saying that the best things in life are free:

To live content with small means;
To seek elegance rather than luxury,
And refinement rather than fashion;
To be worthy, not respectable, and wealthy, not rich;
To study hard, think quietly, talk gently, act frankly;
To listen to stars and birds,
To babes and sages with open heart;
To bear all cheerfully, do all bravely,
Await occasions, hurry never.
In a word, to let the spiritual, unbidden and unconscious,
Grow up through the common.
This is to be my symphony.[8]

The Phillips translation of the Bible offers this rendering of Philippians 1:9-11:

> My prayer for you is that you may have still more love – a love that is full of knowledge and wise insight. I want you to be able always to recognize the highest and the best, and to live sincere and blameless lives until the day of Christ. I want to see your lives full of true goodness, produced by the power that Jesus Christ gives you to the praise and glory of God.

Give God the Fat

God wants first place in our lives today, just as He demanded the best that the Israelites had to offer. He commanded Moses:

> Out of all your gifts you shall present every offering due to the Lord, from all the best of them, the sacred part from them. You shall say to them, "When you have offered from it the best of it, then the rest shall be reckoned to the Levites as the product of the threshing floor, and as the product of the wine vat (Numbers 18:29-30 NASB).

Because the fat was the choicest part of the animal, all the fat was God's (Leviticus 3:16). The firstfruits of all their produce also belonged to Him, as well as the firstborn of all their cattle. Even the firstborn child had to be redeemed or bought back from God with money (Numbers 18:12-16). Giving God their best required sacrifice, but it proved to be a blessing. In this regard God encouraged them to put Him to the test, saying,

> "Bring the whole tithe into the storehouse, so that there may be food in My house, and test Me now in this," says the Lord of hosts, "if I will not open for you the windows of heaven and pour out for you a blessing until it overflows" (Malachi 3:10 NASB).

The churches of Macedonia (where Philippi was located) were not bound by the Law of Moses because it had been abolished at the cross. But they did practice sacrificial giving by first giving themselves to the Lord (2 Corinthians 8:5). This is what God desires of us – that we give Him our very best. To do that, we must guard our hearts and minds.

Questions to Chew On

1. Under the Law of Moses, what did "the fat" of a thing signify? What does it mean to give God the fat?

2. Name some safety guidelines for handling food. What spiritual applications can we draw?

3. Many of the regulations in the Law of Moses are recognized as healthy today. Name a few.

4. What is sanctification?

5. From what have Christians been called?

6. To what extent should a Christian woman resemble the world in her dress, behavior and speech?

7. List three of your favorite pastimes. How do they measure up to Philippians 4:8?

8. What are some of the benefits of media? The dangers?

9. The best things in life are free. Name a few.

10. Name some things that giving God our best might involve.

FOOD *for* THOUGHT

"Behold, to obey is better than sacrifice, And to heed than the fat of rams"
(1 Samuel 15:22).

TAKE OUT

*Keeping clean between the ears may be more important
than keeping clean behind the ears.*

PRAYER *List*

_____

_____

_____

_____

_____

_____

_____

_____

_____

_____

_____

_____

_____

_____

_____

_____

_____

_____

_____

MILK

Milk has been called "nature's most nearly perfect food." Dieticians tell us it is the one food for which there seems to be no adequate substitute. This is because it contains some of all the nutrients the body needs: carbohydrates, fats, minerals, proteins and vitamins. Milk is an important part of most adults' diets, and it is the first food of all newborn babies, whether breast-fed or bottle-fed.

Most of our milk comes from cows, but goat's milk is preferred by some people. Plant-derived soy or rice "milk" is not, technically, real milk although it is marketed as such. People in Bible times often drank milk from goats, sheep and camels. Goat's milk, carried in a skin slung over one's back, would quickly sour and turn into what was considered a very refreshing drink like our buttermilk. Camel's milk, we are told, was rich, strong and not too sweet.[1]

The land God promised Israel was described as a place that flowed with "milk and honey" (Joshua 5:6). God provided these blessings initially, but the people had to preserve them. Proverbs 27:23-27 advised the Israelites to take good care of their flocks. By doing this they would always have a steady supply of goat's milk to feed their households.

Buttermilk Bread

Ingredients
2 packages active dry yeast
½ cup warm water (110 degrees)
½ cup butter or margarine
1½ cups buttermilk
¼ cup white sugar
2 teaspoons salt
½ teaspoon baking soda
5½ cups bread flour

Directions
Dissolve yeast in warm water. Place the butter or margarine and buttermilk in a small saucepan. Heat slowly until butter has melted. Cool to lukewarm. Place sugar, salt, baking soda, buttermilk mixture and dissolved yeast in large mixing bowl. Add 3 cups flour one cup at a time, and mix with the dough hook attachment of an electric mixer. Gradually add the remaining flour while continuing to mix.

When dough is not sticky, turn out on a lightly floured surface. Knead for several minutes until the dough is soft and smooth. Place in a greased bowl and turn once. Allow to rise until doubled in size. Punch down the dough. Divide, and shape into 2 loaves. Place in two well-greased 8-by-4-inch bread pans. Allow to rise until dough has risen one inch above pans. Bake in a preheated 375-degree oven for 30 to 35 minutes. Loaves are done when nicely brown and hollow-sounding when thumped. Yield: 2 loaves.

I Pet 2:2
I Cor. 3:2

CHAPTER 9

PURE MILK
OF THE WORD

Paul wrote in 1 Corinthians 7:15 that "God has called us to peace." That is because He is a God not of confusion but of peace (14:33). Notice these passages:

- "[T]o be spiritually minded is life and peace" (Romans 8:6).
- "Now the God of peace be with you all" (Romans 15:33).
- "For [Christ]) Himself is our peace" (Ephesians 2:14).
- "And let the peace of God rule in your hearts" (Colossians 3:15).
- "Now may the God of peace Himself sanctify you completely" (1 Thessalonians 5:23).
- "Now may the Lord of peace Himself continually give you peace in every way" (2 Thessalonians 3:16).

Clearly peace is available, but how do we access it?

Peace Like a River

Isaiah 66 contains a prophecy that is generally understood to refer to the church. In it a woman called Zion (Jerusalem) gives birth to a son who immediately becomes a nation (v. 7-8). The child is nourished on his mother's milk and is filled with peace. The passage says,

> For thus says the Lord, "Behold, I extend peace to her like a river, And the glory of the nations like an overflowing stream; And you will be nursed, you will be carried on the hip and fondled on the knees. As one whom his mother comforts, so I will comfort you; And you will be comforted in Jerusalem" (Isaiah 66:12-13 NASB).

This "peace like a river" would flow from the milk on which the infant church would be nourished.

Nourished in the Word

In most cultures a newborn baby is laid immediately upon its mother's breast to nurse, and this is the picture that is painted in 1 Peter 1:23-2:2: "[F]or you have been born again ... Therefore ... like newborn babies, long for the pure milk of the word, so that by it you may grow in respect to salvation" (NASB). He used a term that signifies an intense longing to be fed. A new Christian finds satisfaction in learning the first principles of the gospel – things concerning faith, repentance and baptism, among others (Hebrews 6:1-2). She is not yet ready for more difficult teachings because she needs time to digest what God's Word says about these fundamental truths. Paul wrote to the young church at Corinth saying, "I fed you with milk and not solid food; for until now you were not able to receive it" (1 Corinthians 3:2).

NOURISH

verb – to feed or sustain with substances necessary to life and growth.

While a healthy appetite is the normal reaction of a newborn, occasionally one will show a disinterest in feeding. When this happens the child can become sickly and suffer from a condition known as "failure to thrive." Death can result unless measures are taken to see that the baby is properly nourished. Unfortunately, new Christians sometimes suffer from the same poor appetite, and if they are not nurtured by those who are more spiritually mature, they also will become weak and may experience a premature death.

As babes in Christ begin to cut their spiritual teeth, they gradually become able to digest more solid food, and eventually they will learn how to feed themselves. A nourishing diet during these critical years does more than cause steady growth. It also satisfies and makes for a happy and contented child. In the same way, regular feeding upon the Word results in peace and contentment for the child of God.

Marking One's Growth

Most moms and dads keep a growth chart somewhere, recording how their child is progressing. It may be in the baby book or even on a closet door. That chart measures the inches and pounds the child has gained in a year's time. It's an indication of healthy and steady growth, which is the expectation of every loving parent. Watching her child grow brings great satisfaction to a mother. Hannah must have observed with pride how her young Samuel was developing on each of her yearly visits to the tabernacle (1 Samuel 1:7; 2:19, 26). Mary also took note of how Jesus was maturing as a youth, and it warmed her heart (Luke 2:51-52).

Is it not natural, then, that our heavenly Father is concerned about the spiritual growth of His children? He delights in seeing us develop into mature Christians, but this can only happen when we are getting proper nourishment from the Word. With such easy access to the written Word, there is little excuse for stunted growth.

First-century Christians did not have their own copies of Scripture from which to read. They had to rely upon the oral teachings of those who were inspired by God as well as the written epistles they received. Special gifts of the Holy Spirit were given to some, equipping them to serve as apostles, prophets, evangelists, pastors and teachers so that the body of Christ could grow to maturity (Ephesians 4:11-16). Paul, therefore, urged the brethren to give close attention to the things they had heard and learned from him. He wrote, "The things which you learned and received and heard and saw in me, these do, and the God of peace will be with you" (Philippians 4:9).

Got Milk?

The Hebrews writer advised that everyone who partakes only of milk is still a babe. Something is wrong when the appetite fails to grow with the body. Solid food is needed by those who are mature (Hebrews 5:13-14). But while some would stay on milk forever, others stop drinking it altogether. A popular series of advertisements, featuring celebrities sporting liquid mustaches, asked the question, "Got milk?" It was a subtle reminder that we never outgrow the need for milk – regardless of our age.

Isaiah wrote about those who fill up on costly junk food when the pure milk of God's Word is available for free:

> Come, everyone who thirsts, come to the waters; and he who has no money, come, buy and eat! Come, buy wine and milk without money and without price. Why do you spend your money for that which is not bread, and your labor for that which does not satisfy? Listen diligently to me, and eat what is good, and delight yourselves in rich food. Incline your ear, and come to me; hear, that your soul may live; and I will make with you an everlasting covenant, my steadfast, sure love for David (Isaiah 55:1-3 ESV).

Get Your RDA

Becoming a healthy child of God should be the goal of each one of us. Paul told the Ephesian brethren that growing up in Christ makes for a strong body.

> Rather, speaking the truth in love, we are to grow up in every way into him who is the head, into Christ, from whom the whole body, joined and held together by every joint with which it is equipped, when each part

is working properly, makes the body grow so that it builds itself up in love (Ephesians 4:15-16 ESV).

No other food approaches milk in its calcium content, which is necessary for building strong bones. To ensure proper growth we need to follow the recommended daily allowance of milk in our diet. We women need two or three servings each day to meet our calcium need, and we can get it in various ways – in cheese, yogurt, etc. More to the point, we need to ask ourselves, "Am I getting my RDA (recommended daily allowance) of milk from the Word?" There are different ways to do that, too.

We must recognize that Christian women should study the Word just as diligently as Christian men. Although our place is not in the pulpit, we are to become teachers. Paul advised Timothy, "And the things that you have heard from me among many witnesses, commit these to faithful men who will be able to teach others also" (2 Timothy 2:2).

The word used here for "men" is the Greek *anthropois,* which means "people." It is the same root from which we get our English word "anthropology." Women are the first teachers at whose knees children learn, and throughout life many opportunities will arise for us to share the gospel. In order to do that, we must first become students ourselves. Like the Bereans to whom Paul preached, we should examine the Scriptures daily (Acts 17:10-11). A close study of the Bible will aid us in answering the questions that may trouble people most often:

- Where did I come from?
- What is my purpose for living?
- What will become of me when I die?
- How do I determine what is right and wrong?
- How can I make the most of my life?

Every woman needs a place where she can go in solitude to receive some daily nourishment from the Word. Perhaps you have a spare room or a nook that can function as a study – even a kitchen table. Find some place that is comfortable and quiet and inviting. Some would call it a "sacred space." Gradually invest in a few necessary tools, such as a complete concordance, a Bible atlas, a Bible dictionary or encyclopedia, and perhaps a few commentaries. You might draw up a "wish list" and request study books as gifts. Become part of a ladies' Bible class, and subscribe to brotherhood journals and periodicals. Whenever possible, take in lectureships and workshops. Many offer classes geared specifically to the needs of women. This may sound overwhelming, but don't be intimidated. Do what you can, and you will find that the more you study, the more your appetite for learning will increase.

It is often said that the church is always one generation away from apostasy. Many see a crisis today involving biblical illiteracy in America – and not just in the culture generally, but in our churches as well. A once-strong people can become "rickety" without proper nourishment. While skim milk may be recommended for those on a calorie-restricted diet, it is not recommended when it comes to spiritual growth. Neither is a steady diet of condensed milk, which has a high-sugar content. What our world needs is the "whole" milk of God's Word rather than a message that has been watered down or laced with sugar (Acts 20:27).

Milk in the Recipe

All the dry ingredients in our bread recipe – the flour, sugar, salt and yeast – are activated by the liquid of the milk. In the same way, the Word of God is intended to touch and influence every part of our lives. Milk may be nature's most *nearly* perfect food, but God's Word is absolutely perfect. In this world, there is no equal (Psalm 19:7).

Questions to Chew On

1. Why might the Promised Land have been described as a land "flowing with milk and honey"?

2. Why does Peter compare new Christians to babies on a diet of milk?

3. What responsibilities do mature Christians have toward babes in Christ?

4. What happens to a child who stays on a diet of milk only?

5. Name some ways we can mark our spiritual growth.

6. Are you more spiritually mature today than you were five years ago?

7. Do we ever outgrow our need for some milk? Why should we frequently restudy some "first principles"?

8. Discuss the role of women as teachers.

9. Is America becoming biblically illiterate? Discuss.

10. Review some ways in which God's Word is similar to milk.

FOOD *for* THOUGHT

*"[B]e a good servant of Christ Jesus, con-
stantly nourished on the words of the faith
and of the sound doctrine which you have
been following"* (1 Timothy 4:6 NASB).

TAKE OUT

The milk of human kindness never curdles.

PRAYER *List*

Kim Marshall,
Dale Gladdin - his wife
milt
Mike & Janine
Micheal Blass

THE STARTER

Women in Bible times made their bread by mixing flour meal with salt and water or some other liquid, then leaving the dough to rise in the sun. Leavening, or rising of the dough, took place because of natural contaminants in the meal, such as wild yeast and other bacteria. These contaminants caused the meal to ferment when the liquid was added, producing bubbles of carbon dioxide gas. Because yeast-producing bacteria are found in many foods, including milk, fruits and vegetables, different strains of yeast developed. Through trial and error, women learned which combinations produced the best kind of yeast. These strains, called "starters," were then handed down from generation to generation.

Every new bride would have brought a portion of the starter from her mother's house to her house, and she would have guarded it carefully. For each batch of bread she baked, she used a small portion of the starter and "fed" the rest with more flour and liquid so that it continued to grow.

Ancient Egyptian hieroglyphs include pictures of this process; it is believed that yeast has been used for thousands of years. Once scientists had discovered the yeast bacteria at work, they were able to market products such as baking soda, baking powder and active dry yeast. All these products have made our baking much easier, but many women still enjoy making their bread with a starter they received from a friend. In this way they keep alive a practice almost as old as time itself.

Friendship Starter Bread

This recipe begins with a batch of starter dough from a friend. Keep the initial starter in the refrigerator for 3 to 5 days. Take out and feed with the following: ¾ cup sugar; 3 tablespoons instant potatoes; and 1 cup warm water. Mix well and add to the starter. After mixing, let the starter stand out of the refrigerator 8 to 12 hours.

Remove 1 cup of the starter to use in making bread, and return the remaining starter to the refrigerator for 3 to 5 days before feeding again. If you are not making bread after feeding, give or throw away 1 cup. *The starter must be fed every five days to increase the bulk.*

In a large bowl make a stiff batter using ½ cup sugar; 1 teaspoon salt; 1 cup starter; 1½ cups warm water; and 6 cups of sifted bread flour.

Grease a large bowl; put dough in it, and turn over to oil all sides. Cover with waxed paper, and let stand overnight. *Do not refrigerate.*

The next morning, push down and place dough on a lightly floured board and knead a little. Divide into 3 parts, and knead each part again. Place in 3 greased and floured loaf pans, and cover lightly with waxed paper. Let rise slowly 4 to 5 hours.

Bake on bottom rack of the oven at 300 to 350 degrees for 30-40 minutes. Remove and brush with butter while hot. Bread can be frozen. Yield: 3 loaves.

CHAPTER 10

THE LEAVENING OF OPTIMISM

Do you ever wish you knew what a particular Bible character looked like? What did Jesus look like? We can only guess that He was an ordinary-looking Jewish male. One Messianic reference mentions His beard, but Isaiah wrote that nothing was so unusual about His appearance that it would draw people to Him (Isaiah 50:6; 53:2). We know that God directs us to consider a person's heart rather than his or her outward appearance, as 1 Samuel 16:7 teaches. So it is probably for this very reason that no record of Jesus' physical attributes is given.

Paul is another person who stirs our imagination. One second-century writer imagined Paul as a man who was small of build, bald and bow-legged. Because this account is probably fictional, it is of little help in picturing him accurately. What we *do* know, however, is what Paul revealed about himself. He wrote about his stay in Corinth as a time of weakness and fear. He sometimes trembled, and his speech and preaching "were not with persuasive words of human wisdom" (1 Corinthians 2:3-4). He added that he often was poorly clothed, and he knew what it was like to be hungry and thirsty. His critics in the city slandered him and treated him like "filth," to use Paul's words (4:10-13). They complained that his speech was contemptible (2 Corinthians 10:10). In nearby Athens, a group of learned philosophers ridiculed him, calling him a "babbler" (Acts 17:18). A Roman governor in Jerusalem even dismissed him as "mad," claiming Paul was out of his mind (Acts 26:24). No doubt, a great deal of these criticisms were leveled by people who were simply convicted by his preaching. Still, it would have taken a strong individual not to become discouraged by such put-downs.

It does seem that Paul was afforded more respect by some people before he became a Christian. He remembered his former life as a time when his future looked promising, saying:

> If anyone else thinks he may have confidence in the flesh, I more so: circumcised the eighth day, of the stock of Israel, of the tribe of Benjamin, a Hebrew of the Hebrews; concerning the law, a Pharisee; concerning zeal, persecuting the church; concerning the righteousness which is in the law, blameless" (Philippians 3:4-6).

> And I advanced in Judaism beyond many of my contemporaries in my own nation, being more exceedingly zealous for the traditions of my fathers (Galatians 1:14).

Paul might even have been well off, for he told the Philippians that he had experienced humble means as well as prosperity (Philippians 4:12). The only credentials he took any pride in, however, were the ones mentioned in 2 Corinthians 11. And those he told about reluctantly, mentioning them only because his qualifications as an apostle had been questioned. He wrote:

> Since many boast according to the flesh, I will boast also ... Are they Hebrews? So am I. Are they Israelites? So am I. Are they descendants of Abraham? So am I. Are they servants of Christ? – I speak as if insane – I more so; in far more labors, in far more imprisonments, beaten times without number, often in danger of death. Five times I received from the Jews thirty-nine lashes.

Three times I was beaten with rods, once I was stoned, three times I was shipwrecked, a night and a day I have spent in the deep. I have been on frequent journeys, in dangers from rivers, dangers from robbers, dangers from my countrymen, dangers from the Gentiles, dangers in the city, dangers in the wilderness, dangers on the sea, dangers among false brethren; I have been in labor and hardship, through many sleepless nights, in hunger and thirst, often without food, in cold and exposure. Apart from such external things, there is the daily pressure upon me of concern for all the churches" (2 Corinthians 11:18, 22-28 NASB).

Finally, in Galatians is the suggestion that Paul suffered from poor vision (4:13-15; 6:11). These details lead us to imagine a body worn with hardships of many kinds, and they add to our mental picture of what Paul might have looked like. Couple that image with his mention of chains (Philippians 1:7, 14, 16), and we might expect – did we not know Paul better – that he would be a broken old man, one given to depression. But this was not the case. While all these circumstances might leave some people bitter, Paul was content.

- "Not that I speak in regard to need, for I have learned in whatever state I am, to be content" (Philippians 4:11).

- "Therefore I am well content with weaknesses, with insults, with distresses, with persecutions, with difficulties, for Christ's sake; for when I am weak, then I am strong" (2 Corinthians 12:10 NASB).

- "Now godliness with contentment is great gain ... And having food and clothing, with these we shall be content" (1 Timothy 6:6, 8).

The secret of Paul's remarkable attitude is revealed in Philippians 3:7-11. There he said:

But what things were gain to me, these I have counted loss for Christ. But indeed I also count all things loss

118 · A Recipe for Peace

for the excellence of the knowledge of Christ Jesus my Lord, for whom I have suffered the loss of all things, and count them as rubbish, that I may gain Christ and be found in Him, not having my own righteousness, which is from the law, but that which is through faith in Christ, the righteousness which is from God by faith; that I may know Him and the power of His resurrection, and the fellowship of His sufferings, being conformed to His death, if, by any means, I may attain to the resurrection from the dead (Philippians 3:7-11).

Paul could accept the hardships of life because he had something so much more wonderful to look forward to. Even facing the possibility of death, he knew better days lay ahead, so he wrote, "For to me, to live is Christ, and to die is gain" (Philippians 1:21).

The Yeast of Optimism

Paul's contentment was proof of an optimistic outlook. Optimism is the yeast in our recipe for peace. It is the attitude that allows our spirits to rise during times of distress. This can happen because, as Winston Churchill once said, "A pessimist sees the difficulty in every opportunity; an optimist sees the opportunity in every difficulty." Such was true of Paul, who saw in his imprisonment a great opportunity for furthering the gospel. He told the brethren not to worry about him, explaining, "But I want you to know, brethren, that the things which happened to me have actually turned out for the furtherance of the gospel" (Philippians 1:12). He went on to relate that the whole palace guard in Rome had come to understand that he was chained for the cause of Christ. Not only that, but many Christians had begun to preach the gospel with more boldness because of his example (vv. 13-14). That is the outlook of an optimist.

Dealing With Worry

Thinking optimistically is impossible if we let ourselves become consumed with worry. Jesus taught this in the Sermon on the Mount when He said:

> "Therefore I say to you, do not worry about your life, what you will eat or what you will drink; not about your body, what you will put on. Is not life more than food and the body more than clothing? ... For after all these things the Gentiles seek. For your heavenly Father knows that you need all these things. But seek first the kingdom of God and His righteousness, and all these things shall be added to you. Therefore do not worry about tomorrow, for tomorrow will worry about its own things. Sufficient for the day is its own trouble" (Matthew 6:25, 32-34).

The meaning here, according to the Greek, is not that we can never be concerned about our circumstances. Paul himself said that he had daily concerns for the churches he had established (2 Corinthians 11:28). Jesus' warning was against constant worry that does not allow for confidence in God's providential care. Therefore, Paul told the Philippians to be "anxious for nothing," turning everything over to God in prayer (Philippians 4:6). Doing this will allow the peace of God to guard our hearts and minds.

Harmful Yeast

Can you imagine the impact it would have had upon the Philippian brethren if Paul had complained to them about his circumstances? Instead of commending them for their giving through the years, suppose Paul had criticized them for the times when they had not been able to support him (Philippians 4:10). Suppose he had taken the opportunity to rant about other churches that had neglected him altogether? What if Paul had thrown a pity party in describing his imprisonment or condemned them for the fact that problems had arisen in their fellowship? Had he done these things, his letter would have been counterproductive, having a negative impact rather than an encouraging one. Our attitudes and actions, then, can affect others in a negative way. Jesus pointed this out to His disciples, saying, "Take heed and beware of the leaven of the Pharisees and the Sadducees," referring to their harmful teachings (Matthew 16:6, 11).

Just a bit of yeast is all that is needed to leaven a whole lump of dough (1 Corinthians 5:6). In the same way, one person's negative attitudes can affect many other people in a disproportionate way. Some studies have shown that our brains are more responsive to unpleasant words than to positive ones, and that's why negative comments stay with us longer than positive ones. Experts say that at least two positive comments are needed to offset each negative one; and when it comes to married couples, the ratio is five-to-one.

Perhaps this is why Paul was so eager for his "true companion," whose identity is unclear (Philippians 4:3), to help the two women, Euodia and Syntyche, with their differences. Like a couple of bad potatoes in a bin, their problem had the potential to affect the entire church with discouragement.

"I Can" Attitude

Paul's letter must have been encouraging to his friends. It certainly has had that effect upon readers through the years who often cite the words of Philippians 4:13 as a favorite Bible verse: "I can do all things through Christ who strengthens me." His words demonstrate an "I can" attitude. Notice what he writes in verses 11-13: "I have learned … I know … I have learned … I can." Like "starter" yeast, these words have been passed down through many generations, blessing all who have been encouraged by them and, in turn, have shared them with others.

Questions to Chew On

1. How did Bible women leaven their bread?

2. Name some circumstances in Paul's life that could have been depressing.

3. What did weakness do for Paul (2 Corinthians 12:10)?

4. How did he deal with the prospect of death?

5. Quote Churchill's definition of the optimist and the pessimist.

6. What did Jesus teach about worry?

7. Distinguish between worry and concern.

8. How do negative people affect their families? Their coworkers? Their congregations?

9. How is optimism similar to leaven?

10. Why do you suppose Philippians 4:13 is so often quoted?

FOOD for THOUGHT

"Let your conduct be without covetousness; and be content with such things as you have. For He Himself has said, 'I will never leave you nor forsake you' "
(Hebrews 13:5).

TAKE OUT

*"The richest man, whatever his lot, is he who
is content with what he has got."*
– Dutch Proverb

PRAYER *List*

SALT

Without the right concentration of minerals in the body, the heart will not beat normally and the muscles and nerves will not perform as they should. Sodium is one of these necessary minerals, and most people get it by adding salt to their diet. Today, table salt is inexpensive and readily available to everyone. Most of what we see on grocery shelves is mined from underground deposits.

Sea salt, which is considered to be better in quality, is becoming more popular in cooking and is usually more expensive. It is made by evaporating salt water from the sea. The Dead Sea is the source for a great deal of salt-water mining today. In Bible times, people collected sea water from the Dead Sea and other salt-water lakes and allowed it to evaporate in the sun. The natural salt crystals that were left behind supplied what they needed for cooking and other uses.

Ancient civilizations valued salt so highly that it was widely used for trading. Because salt was needed to season food and also to preserve it, areas with large salt deposits grew rich. In the Roman army, soldiers were paid with either a ration of salt or money with which they could buy it. It was so prized that it gave rise to the expression "worth your salt." The Latin word *salarium*, which was used to designate this salt allowance, grew into our English word "salary."

Salt has many other uses besides seasoning food, but its use in cooking is what we think about first. Too much salt can cause health problems such as hypertension (high blood pressure); therefore, for this reason, no more than 2,300 milligrams of salt is recommended per day for most people.[1] This is the equivalent of about 1 teaspoon.

Tips for Cooking With Salt

• If you have over-salted soup, add a peeled, quartered potato for 15 minutes, then discard. Or add a bit of unsalted white rice that has been cooked and pureed into a thin paste. Remember that the liquid in soups is reduced as it simmers, so the salt flavor will intensify as the soup cooks.

• Do not add salt before whipping egg whites. It will increase whipping time and decrease the volume.

• Wait until water boils before adding salt to vegetables and pasta.

• Reducing the salt in bread recipes usually results in sticky dough. Considering the small amount called for, it is not recommended as a rule that you leave it out.

• Seafoods are naturally high in salt, so add more sparingly.

• Do not store salt in silver containers. The chlorine will cause a green discoloration.

• One tablespoon of coarse or kosher salt equals 1 teaspoon table salt.

CHAPTER 11

SEASONED WITH SALT

Have you ever been on a salt-free diet? It takes some getting used to. Even Job complained that food is tasteless without it, saying, "Can something tasteless be eaten without salt, Or is there any taste in the white of an egg? My soul refuses to touch them; They are like loathsome food to me" (Job 6:6-7 NASB). Translators are unclear whether the text is actually referring to an egg or a tasteless plant, but they agree that either one would be bland without salt. Most likely, Job was saying that the advice of his friends was unpalatable and did not appeal to him.

Although we normally associate salt with food, less than 5 percent of all the salt produced in the world each year is used in food. It is estimated that altogether salt has more than 14,000 uses.[2] In the Bible we read about its use in food, as an antiseptic and as a preservative.

• Every grain offering that was brought to God had to be seasoned with salt (Leviticus 2:13).

• Salt was used as an antiseptic at childbirth. Ezekiel 16:4 describes how once a baby's navel cord had been cut, the child was washed and rubbed with salt before being wrapped in cloth. The

International Standard Bible Encyclopedia claims that Arabs of the desert, in the absence of salt, bathe their infants in camels' urine.[3]

• The preservative quality of salt has long been recognized as well. In Scripture this quality is used symbolically to represent things that were intended to be everlasting. Offerings made to Jehovah were called "a covenant of salt forever before the Lord" in Numbers 18:19. Second Chronicles 13:5 also mentions an everlasting covenant of salt between God and David's descendants. In the Arab world, when men ate together they became friends. Their friendship was sealed with the eating of salt; partaking of a man's hospitality and friendship was described as "eating of one's salt."[4]

Jesus and Salt

Two of the gospel accounts record a quotation of Jesus about salt. In both cases He used this symbol to illustrate a person's influence upon others and the way he or she interacts with them. Jesus said to his disciples,

> You are the salt of the earth; but if the salt has become tasteless, how can it be made salty again? It is no longer good for anything, except to be thrown out and trampled under foot by men" (Matthew 5:13 NASB).

> Salt is good; but if the salt becomes unsalty, with what will you make it salty again? Have salt in yourselves, and be at peace with one another (Mark 9:50 NASB).

Notice that the "salt" in these verses represents an attitude that seeks to brings peace to relationships with other people. It is used this way in Colossians 4:6: "Let your speech always be with grace, seasoned with salt, that you may know how you ought to answer each one."

Perhaps Jesus had the preservative quality of salt in mind here, too. We tend to forget that without modern means of refrigeration, our ancestors were limited in how long they could keep food before it spoiled. Under the Law of Moses, food offerings had to be eaten within two days; whatever was left had to be burned on the third day (Leviticus 19:5-6). We only have to go back a few generations to find food being preserved by canning, drying (dehydrating) or salting. In calling His disciples "the salt of the earth," Jesus may have been suggesting that preserving the peace so needed in our world would require each of us to let our influence for good *be felt*.

Salt's Permeating Quality

However salt is used, whether in food, in cleansing or in preservation, it is only effective when it permeates whatever it touches. Clearly, Jesus was teaching that His followers are supposed to make a difference in the world. In telling Christians that we are not to associate with worldly people, Paul had to explain his meaning (1 Corinthians 5:9-13). He was not referring to non-

> ### PRESERVE
>
> *verb – to keep from spoiling or rotting by canning, pickling or salting, etc.*

Christians because, as he writes, we would have to leave this world altogether if that were the case. Rather, he was encouraging the church to practice discipline with members who are guilty of immorality because "a little leaven leavens the whole lump" (v. 6). Jesus taught His disciples to permeate the society around them, saying:

> You are the light of the world. A city that is set on a hill cannot be hidden. Nor do they light a lamp and put it under a basket, but on a lampstand, and it gives light to all who are in the house. Let your light so shine before men, that they may see your good works and glorify your Father in heaven (Matthew 5:14-16).

When James wrote that "friendship with the world is enmity with God," he did not mean that we cannot form friendships with non-Christians. Otherwise, we could never share the gospel with them. In saying that "[w]hoever therefore wants to be a friend of the world makes himself an enemy of God," he meant that we cannot live like the world and serve God at the same time (James 4:4-5). Jesus' closest companions were those of like faith; those were the people He shared His most intimate times with. But He was open to sinners whenever the opportunity arose to share the gospel with them. We need to remember these words often as we think about our personal mission in life:

- "I did not come to call the righteous, but sinners, to repentance" (Matthew 9:13).

- "But God demonstrates His own love toward us, in that while we were still sinners, Christ died for us" (Romans 5:8).

- "This is a faithful saying and worthy of all acceptance, that Christ Jesus came into the world to save sinners, of whom I am chief" (1 Timothy 1:15).

✓ 11·5 The Beauty of Friendship

Some of the most troubled people in the world are those who have no friends. How often do we pick up the newspaper or hear on television about some horrific crime that has been committed by someone described as a "loner." Psychologists tell us that loners often are people who have suffered for a long time from low self-esteem. Unable to cope with the feeling that they are unloved and unworthy, loners attempt to guard their wounded egos in one of several different ways.

James Dobson, in his book *Hide or Seek: How to Build Self-Esteem in Your Child*, describes each of these attempts in detail. These coping mechanisms are: "hiding" within a shell of silence and loneliness; becoming a bully; clowning around; denying reality through the use of drugs, alcohol or fantasy; or simply by conforming to the expectations of others. A sixth and more effective method is compensation. Of them all, compensation is the one solution to loneliness that can be effective. Compensation works on the "I can" principle and resolves to find a positive solution when a person is feeling alone and insecure.[5]

Feelings of isolation are not good. God understood when He

created Adam that it was not good for the man to live alone. That is why He also created Eve, a companion who was suitable for him (Genesis 2:18). We all need friends and companions who will stand by us in difficult situations. Solomon wrote, "Two are better than one, Because they have a good reward for their labor. For if they fall, one will lift up his companion. But woe to him who is alone when he falls, For he has no one to help him up" (Ecclesiastes 4:9-10). Proverbs 17:17 reminds us that "[a] friend loves at all times, And a brother is born for adversity." In other words, good friends will be there when you need them or, as the old English proverb states, "A friend in need is a friend indeed."

Paul's Joy and Crown

Jesus pronounced a blessing upon those who are "persecuted for righteousness' sake" (Matthew 5:10). Of all those whose examples are recorded in the Bible, Paul would rise high on the list. But Paul also experienced loneliness at times. Imprisoned frequently, he sometimes suffered from isolation and persecution. He knew what it was like to have former friends turn on him. In his final letter to Timothy, written from prison shortly before his death, we can sense Paul's need for the presence of faithful friends. He wrote,

> Be diligent to come to me quickly; for Demas has forsaken me, having loved this present world, and has departed for Thessalonica – Crescens for Galatia, Titus for Dalmatia. Only Luke is with me. Get Mark and bring him with you, for he is useful to me for ministry (2 Timothy 4:9-11).

Someone has written that the difference between friends and enemies is this: Friends will love you despite your faults, and enemies will hate you despite your virtues. Paul never saw himself as a perfect man. In fact, in his former life he was, in his own words, "a blasphemer, a persecutor, and an insolent man," the chief of sinners (1 Timothy 1:13, 15). How he treasured those steadfast friends who loved him despite his past! The peace that radiates through Paul's letter to the Philippians was made possible, in part, because of his friends' love and support. One purpose for writing this epistle was to thank loyal brethren for their continued fellowship in the gospel (Philippians 1:3-5; 4:15-16). His love in return is evident in his benediction, "Therefore, my beloved and longed-for brethren, my joy and crown, so stand fast in the Lord, beloved" (4:1).

To Timothy, his "son in the faith" (1 Timothy 1:2), Paul offered this touching tribute:

> But I trust in the Lord Jesus to send Timothy to you shortly, that I also may be encouraged when I know your state. For I have no one like-minded, who will sincerely care for your state. For all seek their own, not the things which are of Christ Jesus. But you know his proven character, that as a son with his father he served with me in the gospel (Philippians 2:19-22).

Solomon wrote that, for some, a friend exists who will stick closer than a brother (Proverbs 18:24). Paul was blessed to have such a friend in Timothy. The Philippian brethren had such a friend in Epaphroditus, their messenger and minister who was longing to return to them (Philippians 2:25-26). Job's friends, on the other hand, proved to be "[m]iserable comforters" in his time of need (Job 16:2). Their friendship was lacking and failed to comfort. If you would know peace, develop a true friend. To do that, Solomon says, you must first be a friend to others (Proverbs 18:24).

Most of us know someone right now who is hurting and needs a shoulder to lean on. Why not make an effort to help fill that need? "Bear one another's burdens," Paul wrote, "and so fulfill the law of Christ" (Galatians 6:2).

Questions to Chew On

1. Do you agree with Job 6:6? *yes*
2. Discuss the origin of our English word "salary."
3. What lesson did Jesus teach using salt?

4. Discuss some common uses for salt and their spiritual applications.

5. Discuss Jesus' statement that "friendship with the world is enmity with God."

6. What is the lesson learned from 1 Corinthians 15:33?

7. What was Jesus' mission, according to Matthew 9:13? Should it be ours also?

8. Do you have a Proverbs 17:17 friend? Share why this person is special.

9. Who were some of Paul's most cherished friends?

10. Share some ways in which congregations can reach out to those who are hurting.

FOOD *for* THOUGHT

"Let each of you look out not only for his own interests, but also for the interests of others" (Philippians 2:4).

TAKE OUT

A friend is one who walks in when the rest of the world walks out.

PRAYER *List*

_____

_____

_____

_____

_____

_____

_____

_____

_____

_____

_____

_____

_____

_____

_____

_____

_____

COUNTING TIME

Understanding time in the Bible requires some knowledge of the difference between Hebrew time and Roman time, which we use. The Hebrew day began at 6 p.m. and lasted for 24 hours. The Romans began their day at midnight and went to the following midnight. Matthew, Mark and Luke use Jewish time. Parts of John seem to be expressing Roman time.

The Hebrews used a lunar calendar consisting of 12 months. The first month of their religious year, Abib, occurred between our March and April. After the Exodus the month was called Nisan. Their months were generally 30 days long, beginning with each new moon. Because this made for a shorter year than a solar calendar would, they occasionally had to add a 13th month to make up the difference.

Every seventh year was a Sabbatical year when the land was allowed to rest (Leviticus 25:1-7). Every 50th year was called the Year of Jubilee. Once again, the land was left to rest and all of it went back to its original owner. Slaves were also set free and debts canceled.

God does not view time as man does. Moses wrote, "For a thousand years in Your sight Are like yesterday when it is past, And like a watch in the night" (Psalm 90:4).

Yeast Biscuits

The nice thing about these biscuits is that they require less preparation time than most yeast breads. You do not have to allow any time for rising before baking. Also, the dough can be kept in a covered bowl in the refrigerator for up to 10 days.

Ingredients
  2 tablespoons sugar
  1 cup shortening
  5 cups flour
  1 package dry yeast
  ½ cup warm water
  ¾ teaspoon baking soda (if using self-rising flour,
      use a scant ½ teaspoon)
  2 cups buttermilk

Directions
  Cut the sugar into the shortening, and combine with the flour. Dissolve the yeast in warm water and set aside. Add baking soda to the buttermilk; then add all the liquids to the flour mixture and stir. Pinch off small amounts of dough, and shape as desired or roll out and cut. Bake at 425 degrees for 10 to 12 minutes. Yield: 2 dozen tea biscuits.

CHAPTER 12

PUTTING IT
ALL TOGETHER

We have looked at seven key ingredients in the recipe for peace. Once we determine to incorporate these attitudes into our lives, we are well on our way to finding the peace of mind the Bible talks about so often. Let's check our stock of these ingredients once more.

- flour of joy – lots of it
- a spoonful of sweetness
- ongoing prayer to bind us to God
- an offering of fat
- pure, whole milk of the Word
- the yeast of optimism
- salt for seasoning

Preparation is all-important in our spiritual growth just as it is in baking. But knowing the ingredients we need is just the beginning. The difference between success and failure in either undertaking is in the details. We must determine how much of something is too much and how little is too little. God's recipe serves as a guide in measuring our actions, but a lot must be learned through practice – trial and error.

Here is where the novice cook may begin to feel insecure. It's time to start putting our ingredients into something, and Paul told us what that something is in Philippians 4:9: "Whatever you have learned or received or heard from me, or seen in me – put it *into practice*. And the God of peace will be with you" (NIV, emphasis added).

Putting faith into practice has always been the most challenging part of Christianity. That's because the Christian life makes demands of us. Growing in Christian maturity takes time, and isn't always easy. In fact, Scripture teaches that we will undergo some heat in the process – but we must remember that heat is necessary in the transformation process that results in peace. So let's proceed … because good things await, and the end result is well worth the effort!

12-3 How Much Is Too Much?

Once we have our ingredients in mind, the question arises: Exactly how much is called for? Too much fat will result in heavy dough. Not enough yeast will keep the dough from rising. This calls for some decision-making.

In our Christian walk we often wish we had someone to tell us "how much is too much." For example, "How far do I go in trying to teach some people?" "Am I overcommitted? Do I really have time to head up three committees and still meet my family's needs?" "Should we lower our contribution while my husband is looking for work?" "Do I buy my child a coat while it is on sale, or do we donate to the visiting missionary?" We realize that many of the decisions we must make every day are not spelled out for us in Scripture.

What the Bible does teach is the importance of moderation. When Paul says in Philippians 4:5, "Let your gentleness be known to all men," he is using the Greek word *epieikes*, often translated as "forbearance" (ASV). Matthew Arnold translated the word as "sweet reasonableness,"[1] as we discussed in Chapter 6. The

Authorized Version uses the word "moderation." All of these words are related in meaning. Moderation, however, implies the avoidance of excess. In other words, it means we must strive for balance and weigh many of our options carefully, considering how the decisions we make might impact others.

Solomon wrote in Ecclesiastes 3:1 that there is an appropriate time for everything that is good and worthwhile (compare vv. 11-12). There is a time to weep, for example, and a time to laugh (v. 4). But either of these can be inappropriate depending upon the situation. Proverbs 25:11 says, "Like apples of gold in settings of silver Is a word spoken in right circumstances" (NASB). But how do we determine what is appropriate in every situation? Perhaps one clue is found in the latter part of Philippians 4:5: "The Lord is at hand." Wristbands printed with the letters "WWJD" became popular in recent years. "What would Jesus do?" is always a good question to ask.

When do I yield my rights to another, and when do I stand firm? Paul addressed this situation in 1 Corinthians 8 when discussing the eating of meats that had been offered to idols. He knew nothing was intrinsically wrong with it and that he could do it in good conscience. But other Christians could not eat these meats without defiling their consciences. Paul's judgment was that each individual should beware, lest his or her personal liberty provide a stumbling block to another (v. 9). As he weighed the options, his decision became clear: "[I]f food makes my brother stumble, I will never again eat meat, lest I make my brother stumble" (v. 13). That is the essence of moderation. When we treat other people with this kind of consideration, even to the point of giving up our own "rights" at times, it has a way of coming back to bless us.

Paul wrote, "[G]ive preference to one another in honor" (Romans 12:10 NASB). Giving in to another's preference can result in a blessing. Sometimes it's worth it to "forbear" and do what is best for the other person – and not only because it's what Jesus taught us to do. It also contributes to our own peace. Proverbs 16:7 says, "When a man's ways please the Lord, He makes even his enemies to be at peace with him," and that is worth a great deal.

Put Your Faith Into Practice

Now is the time to follow the recipe's directions and put our faith into practice. Isn't that what Paul said? "Whatever you have learned or received or heard from me, or seen in me – put it into practice. And the God of peace will be with you" (Philippians 4:9 NIV).

I think it's ironic that many people have fully equipped, state-of-the-art kitchens, and yet they don't like to cook. They never go into the kitchen except to grab a bowl of cereal or plug in the coffee maker. Spices are in the cupboard that have never been opened. A cookbook may even be sitting on the counter. But for all practical purposes, that kitchen is for looks only.

As Christians we must be careful that we aren't merely keeping up appearances. It isn't enough just to attend the services of the church, Bible in hand. How interested are we in learning the basics of what God's Word teaches and really putting them into practice in our everyday lives?

It's time to carry this recipe to completion.

Get Started

Timing is all-important in cooking – especially when making yeast bread because it must be done incrementally. Heat; let the mixture cool. Mix; let the dough rise. Roll it out; let it rise again. There is no hurrying this process. Dough takes its time; the longer you allow it to rise, the better the result will be.

Serving God is much like working with dough. God has His sense of timing, and when we try to rush Him along, things never turn out right. So many examples of this are found in Scripture that you'd think we would learn from them.

Take Abraham and Sarah, for example. God promised Abraham (then called Abram) that He would make of him a great nation (Genesis 12:1-3). Several more times God repeated the promise, telling him that he would have a son (12:7; 13:14-16; 15:1-5). Ten years later Abram was still childless because Sarai, his wife, was barren. Sarai decided that God needed some help, and she gave her handmaid, Hagar, to Abram so that Hagar might produce this promised heir. But this was not God's plan. God waited another 13 years before revealing to Abraham that Sarah herself (as God renamed her) was going to give birth to a child. Abraham thus became the father of two boys instead of one, and their descendants became mortal enemies. They are battling each other to this day – because Sarah and Abraham did not wait for God.

Paul could cite a personal example of God's unique timing. During his third missionary journey, he was making plans to visit Rome after his mission had ended with a brief visit to Jerusalem. He did not know at that point that he would be arrested in Jerusalem and confined for two years in a prison at Caesarea – after which he would be sent to Rome as a prisoner. God's timing was different from Paul's, but it opened unexpected doors for him, as he described in Philippians 1. During the two years Paul was under house arrest at Rome, he had the opportunity to write four inspired letters – Ephesians, Philippians, Colossians and Philemon – something he might not have done otherwise. Had that been the case, we would not be studying the book of Philippians today.

We must remember that God does not view time the way we do and that He is working things according to His purpose Peter wrote that "with the Lord one day is as a thousand years, and a thousand years as one day" (2 Peter 3:8). Seven hundred years passed between Isaiah's vision of the Prince of Peace and His actual appearing "when the fullness of the time had come" (Galatians 4:4). Waiting on the Lord can be difficult, but it always works out best.

Into the Oven

Heating the oven, for most of us, involves a quick turn of the knob and we're done. In Chapter 4 we talked about that control knob. But the process was not so easy for women long ago. Even now, in many parts of the world, preparing the oven is a laborious job that involves cooking outdoors over an open fire.

My Mammy Jackson lived her entire married life in a house without electricity or indoor plumbing. She cooked on a wood-burning stove in the kitchen. I remember eating food as a child that was prepared on that stove, and in my mind it did seem to taste better. I don't think that was necessarily the case, but it just involved so much work that the waiting heightened the anticipation.

Cooking on a wood stove was complicated by today's standards. For one thing, it required plenty of wood – preferably seasoned hardwood that had been stored in the woodpile for several months. Once a load was brought in and placed in the wood box, the fire box in the stove had to be cleaned out. Laying the fire meant layering crumpled paper and a few pieces of dried kindling with the wood on top. Knowing how much to put in was just a matter of trial and error. One also had to be sure the flue was open and the top burners closed. Once the fire was lit, time had to be allowed for it to burn down to the right temperature – again, drawing on experience. Closing the damper made it hotter; opening it lowered the temperature.

> **HEAT**
>
> *noun – a period of excitement, intensity, stress, etc.; the most violent or intense point or stage of something.*

Certain parts of the oven got hotter than other parts, and learning where they were took practice, too. Not every stove cooked the same way. And just imagine, by the time breakfast had been cooked and served, the dishes washed, and the stovetop cleaned, it was time to start all over again.

Why do I mention all of this? Turning a pan of raw dough into mouth-watering hot bread doesn't happen automatically. Dough must go through the heat in order to be transformed into bread. The process isn't easy, and things don't always turn out as expected. Today, by comparison, baking is such a breeze! Set the control knob, turn on the timer and go about your other household chores. It doesn't seem that difficult, but even today the process involves work.

Looking back through the pages of Scripture, we are impressed by the great sacrifices made by so many faithful children of God throughout history. The prophet Isaiah, according to tradition, was sawn in half for his faith. This may be what the Hebrews writer refers to when he writes:

> And what more shall I say? For the time would fail me to tell of Gideon and Barak and Samson and Jephthah, also of David and Samuel and the prophets: who through faith subdued kingdoms, worked righteousness, obtained promises, stopped the mouths of lions, quenched the violence of fire, escaped the edge of the sword, out of weakness were made strong, became valiant in battle, turned to flight the armies of the aliens. Women received their dead raised to life again. Others were tortured, not accepting deliverance, that they might obtain a better resurrection. Still others had trial of mockings and scourgings, yes, and of chains and imprisonment. They were stoned, they were sawn in two, were tempted, were slain with the sword. They wandered about in sheepskins and goatskins, being destitute, afflicted, tormented – of whom the world was not worthy. They wandered in deserts and mountains, in dens and caves of the earth. And all these, having obtained a good testimony through faith, did not receive the promise, God having provided something better for us, that they should not be made perfect apart from us (Hebrews 11:32-40).

What faith is described in these verses! Even Abraham and Sarah, despite their lapse in judgment, gave up much to follow God's call in their lives. To what can we attribute such dedication – such peaceful acceptance of the trials they had to undergo? The Hebrews writer said they had a goal:

> These all died in faith, not having received the promises, but having seen them afar off were assured of

them, embraced them and confessed that they were strangers and pilgrims on the earth (Hebrews 11:13).

Former President Harry Truman is credited with the saying, "If you can't stand the heat, get out of the kitchen." Paul understood that persecution was part of the commitment we must be willing to make when we become Christians. Among his last written words was the warning that "all who desire to live godly in Christ Jesus will suffer persecution" (2 Timothy 3:12). Are we "[r]eady to suffer grief or pain," in the words of an old favorite hymn?[2]

In some parts of the world, Christians still pay dearly for their faith. Some lose their property or are imprisoned, and others pay with their very lives. This is one more way in which most of us are blessed to have life easier than those who went before us. And the sacrifices we *do* make seem small in comparison. That said, our Lord is aware of the hardships each of us must face, and He has promised to help us. He says,

> Come to Me, all you who labor and are heavy laden, and I will give you rest. Take My yoke upon you and learn from Me, for I am gentle and lowly in heart, and you will find rest for your souls. For My yoke is easy and My burden is light (Matthew 11:28-30).

How much heat are we willing to take to become the loaf Christ wants us to be?

Questions to Chew On

1. How does God view time?

2. Think about some things that cause you stress. How is time related?

3. Suggest areas in your life where you find it hard to know how much to do.

4. What does it mean to "give preference to one another"? How do we determine when to do that?

5. What did Jesus teach about "keeping up appearances" in Matthew 23?

6. Discuss the parable in Luke 6:46-49. What is the best preparation for weathering the storms of life?

7. Think about an instance in your life when God's timing was different from yours.

8. Abraham and Sarah misjudged God's timing. What were the consequences?

9. Read and discuss James 1:2-4. Can you relate a time in your life that was painful but eventually resulted in something good?

10. What did Paul predict in 2 Timothy 3:12? Do you believe this?

FOOD *for* THOUGHT

"No temptation [trial] has overtaken you except such as is common to man; but God is faithful, who will not allow you to be tempted beyond what you are able, but with the temptation will also make the way of escape, that you may be able to bear it" (1 Corinthians 10:13).

TAKE OUT

Character, like sweet herbs, should give off its finest fragrance when pressed.

PRAYER *List*

THE PASSOVER FEAST

The Law of Moses required God's people to observe three major feasts every year. They were Passover, which fell in our March or April; Pentecost, which fell in our May or June (also called the Feast of Weeks); and the Feast of Ingathering, which occurred in our September or October. This was also called the Feast of Tabernacles.

The Passover marked the Jews' beginning as a nation, when Moses led the children of Israel out of Egypt. According to God's instructions, on the 10th day of the first month in the Jewish calendar, each household chose a yearling lamb or kid without blemish. The lamb was set aside until the evening of the 14th day, when it was killed. The blood of the lamb was sprinkled upon the doorposts of their houses. "And when I see the blood, I will pass over you," God said (Exodus 12:13). The flesh of the lamb was roasted and eaten that evening with unleavened bread and bitter herbs. The Israelites were to eat it with their sandals on, dressed for travel, and they were commanded to remain in their houses until morning. That evening the Lord passed throughout the land, and in every house upon which there was no blood, the firstborn son died.

The Passover Feast was meant to help the people remember this great event. God had commanded, "So this day shall be to you a memorial; and you shall keep it as a feast to the Lord throughout your generations. You shall keep it as a feast by an everlasting ordinance" (Exodus 12:14). The observance also foreshadowed the death of Jesus, "The Lamb of God who takes away the sin of the world!" (John 1:29). Jesus and His disciples were eating the Passover Feast on the night of His betrayal. It was after this meal that He instituted the Lord's Supper, which became symbolic of His body and blood, sacrificed for the sins of mankind (Luke 22).

Unleavened Bread

Ingredients
2 cups plain flour (Do not use self-rising, or it will not be unleavened.)
5 tablespoons shortening (or oil)
5 tablespoons ice water
A pinch of salt (optional)

Directions
Mix flour and shortening with a fork, adding ice water slowly, a little at a time. Mix until all the flour is moistened and dough forms a ball. (If using a food processor, blend for several seconds or just until dough is mealy.)

Place dough in the refrigerator until cold. Divide into thirds and roll out on lightly floured board. Roll out very thin and cut dough into circles or squares about 4 inches in diameter.*

Place on ungreased cookie sheet and prick all over with a fork. Bake at 300 degrees until done. Bubbles may form, so remove from the oven every 5 to 10 minutes and push down. Yield: enough for 200 people

* A metal hair pick to use just for this purpose works well for tracing out a grid on dough cut into squares.

CHAPTER 13

WELL DONE!

A nticipation runs high as you watch your homemade bread through the oven's glass door. Slowly it turns a golden brown, and a tantalizing aroma fills the kitchen, then the whole house. At the sound of a familiar "ding," you know the wait is up, and you are salivating! The bread is ready to eat. After taking your loaf from the oven, you will want to lavish it with melted butter and serve immediately. Get ready for the praise! Hot yeast bread dipped in butter is a meal unto itself.

Making homemade bread requires time and effort. It really is easier to open a ready-made package and pop it in the oven, but the end result of bread from scratch is so much better. Your family will appreciate your work in going the extra mile for them.

Called to Serve

Going beyond the call of duty is what Christ encourages us to do. It was the focus of His Sermon on the Mount as recorded in Matthew 5:38-48. There He taught a principle that guided His earthly ministry – giving of ourselves, when our actions are motivated by love, causes us to resemble our Heavenly Father.

On occasion, Jesus found it necessary to remind His disciples of that, saying that "the Son of Man did not come to be served, but to serve, and to give His life a ransom for many" (Matthew 20:28).

Women, as a rule, understand service. Most mothers make a career of it. Middle-aged women in "the sandwich generation" often balance rearing children with the needs of elderly parents. Married or single, many women tend homes, hold down jobs, manage finances, and serve as role models in their communities. The worthy woman described in Proverbs 31 did all these things and more, earning a reputation as one who did not eat the bread of idleness. She was praised by her children, her husband and her neighbors because she found joy in going the extra mile.

Blessed in Our Giving

When Paul (then Saul) was converted to Christ, he embarked upon a life that would be characterized by self-sacrifice, even calling himself a "bondservant of Christ." A chosen vessel in the eyes of Jesus, he devoted his life to sharing the gospel with others, including the Philippian brethren to whom he wrote, "if I am being poured out as a drink offering on the sacrifice and service of your faith, I am glad and rejoice with you all" (Philippians 2:17). What motivated Paul to sacrifice so much?

The answer is found in the parable Jesus told about a merchant who dealt in beautiful pearls. Upon finding one pearl that excelled all the others in value, he sold everything he had to buy it (Matthew 13:45-46). He was content to give up all he had because of the surpassing value of what he had found. That is how Paul felt about his life in Christ. It is why he wrote, "For I consider that the sufferings of this present time are not worthy to be compared with the glory which shall be revealed in us" (Romans 8:18).

In his closing remarks of Philippians 4, Paul wrote these words: "Indeed I have all and abound. I am full" (v. 18). It is true that Paul was responding here to gifts sent to him by the church at Philippi, but his words suggest a confidence in God's providential care. He encouraged his friends to trust in God's care also: "And my God shall supply all *your* need according to His riches in glory by Christ Jesus" (v. 19, emphasis added). Paul's confidence was born out of a realization that God had blessed him in the past and would continue to do so. He knew that his Father possessed riches beyond measure – a fact that he alluded to often in his writings:

- The riches of God's goodness, forbearance and long-suffering (Romans 2:4)
- The riches of His glory (Romans 9:23; Ephesians 3:16)
- God's richness for all who call upon Christ (Romans 10:12)
- The depth of the riches of God's wisdom and knowledge (Romans 11:33)
- The riches of His grace (Ephesians 1:7; 2:7)
- The richness of His mercy (Ephesians 2:4)
- The riches of the glory of His inheritance in the saints (Ephesians 1:18)
- The unsearchable riches of Christ (Ephesians 3:8)

Despite hardships and persecution, Paul knew that he had been blessed with "every spiritual blessing in the heavenly places in Christ" (Ephesians 1:3) and fortified by the peace of God.

Lavished With Grace

TV's Paula Deen is known for her love of butter. She uses it generously, lavishing it upon almost everything she cooks. She has been quoted as saying, "You know it's a good recipe if it starts with a stick of butter."

LAVISH
verb – to give generously or liberally

The word "lavished" suggests generosity and liberality, an appropriate word to describe God's goodness toward those who submit to His will. The New American Standard translation uses the word in Ephesians 1:7-8: "In Him we have redemption through His blood, the forgiveness of our trespasses, according to the riches of His grace which He lavished on us." The New International Version uses the same word in 1 John 3:1, "How great is the love the Father has lavished on us, that we should be called children of God!" It is no wonder that Paul said with confidence, "I have all and abound" (Philippians 4:18).

The Rest of the Story

At the time of Paul's writing to the church at Philippi, he expected that he would soon be released from confinement in Rome (Philippians 2:24). According to Luke's account in Acts 28:30, the imprisonment lasted two years, which leads us to believe that he was released at the end of that period. Then, according to tradition and some references in his final epistles, Paul was able to travel for a while and to write the books of 1 and 2 Timothy and Titus.

But freedom was short-lived. Paul was apprehended again, probably because he persisted in preaching the gospel. Apparently he was arrested suddenly, for valuable possessions were left behind in Troas. Back in Rome and confined this time to a prison for the condemned, Paul wrote to Timothy and urged him to come quickly and to bring with him his cloak along with some books and parchments (2 Timothy 4:9, 13). "The time of my departure is at hand," he wrote (v. 6).

With death a certainty, Paul contemplated his decision, years earlier, to serve Jesus. He had no regrets – only a confident expectation that he was going on to better things. He wrote,

> I have fought a good fight, I have finished the race, I have kept the faith. Finally, there is laid up for me the crown of righteousness, which the Lord, the righteous Judge, will give to me on that Day, and not to me only but also to all who have loved His appearing (2 Timothy 4:7-8).

In a previous letter Paul described his view of death in simple terms: the loosening of stakes when a tent is taken down. He wrote, "For we know that if our earthly house, this tent, is destroyed ["torn down" NASB], we have a building from God, a house not made with hands, eternal in the heavens" (2 Corinthians 5:1). Paul was headed home!

Like the hard-working servant in one of Jesus' parables, the apostle was confident that he would receive a warm welcome for all his labors. He expected a commendation from His Lord, and, with it, a reward. In the days before his death, Paul perhaps remembered these words of Jesus, spoken while He remained on the earth: "Well done, good and faithful servant; you were faithful over a few things, I will make you ruler over many things. Enter into the joy of your lord"(Matthew 25:21).

Sweet Peace, the Gift of God's Love

God continues to lavish wonderful gifts upon His children today. Several of the gifts that Paul enumerated are as follows:

- His grace (2 Corinthians 9:14-15)
- The Holy Spirit, given to the obedient believer at baptism (Acts 2:38)
- Talent and ability (Romans 12:6; 1 Timothy 4:14; 1 Peter 4:10)
- Salvation (Ephesians 2:8)
- Eternal life (Romans 6:23)

Certainly we would add the gift of peace, which we have focused on in this study.

Some of the last words of Jesus, spoken to His apostles, were words of peace and comfort: "These things I have spoken to you, that in Me you may have peace" (John 16:33). These words were uttered as Jesus reclined at the table with the eleven, Judas having left to carry out his act of betrayal.

After the observance of the Passover meal, which the twelve ate together, Jesus instituted a memorial feast we know as "the Lord's Supper." He took the unleavened bread, which was always served at Passover, and gave it a new significance.

And He took bread, gave thanks and broke it, and gave it to them, saying, "This is My body which is given for you; do this in remembrance of Me." Likewise He also took the cup after super, saying, "This cup is the new covenant in My blood, which is shed for you" (Luke 22:19-20).

Every Lord's Day since, Christians have assembled to partake of unleavened bread and the cup that signifies Jesus' blood. We do it in remembrance of Him – the Lamb without spot or blemish whose blood was shed for the sins of the world. As we partake, we also anticipate His return (1 Corinthians 11:26). The promise of His return is recorded this way in John 14:2-3, "I go to prepare a place for you. And if I go and prepare a place for you, I will come again and receive you to Myself; that where I am, there you may be also."

Jesus' beautiful benediction continues to offer hope and peace to every faithful believer. "Peace I leave with you, My peace I give to you," He tells us (John 14:27). His is a perfect peace – foreseen by Isaiah the prophet, celebrated by angels at His birth and proclaimed by the apostle Paul.

Think the recipe is too difficult? He is ready to help at every step – the simmering, the sifting, the blending and the folding. Let Him take you through the heat and lavish you with His perfect peace all the way to the final commendation, "Well done!"

Questions to Chew On

1. Recall your decision to become a Christian. Name something you had to give up in order to follow Christ.

2. Why did Jesus choose to be known as a servant?

3. Read Matthew 20:25-28 from several translations. How is this teaching contrary to human nature?

4. How did Paul feel about the sufferings he experienced (Romans 8:18)?

5. Think of some difficult things you have endured. What brought you peace?

6. Is it likely that Paul was released from his confinement shortly after writing the book of Philippians? What evidence is there? What happened to him later?

7. Describe Paul's attitude as he faced death. What are your thoughts?

8. What picture is depicted in 2 Corinthians 5:1?

9. Name some things God has lavished upon Christians. What comforts has He lavished upon you?

10. Whatever problems you are experiencing, do you believe that peace in possible in your life?

FOOD *for* THOUGHT

"And God is able to make all grace abound toward you, that you, always having all sufficiency in all things, may have an abundance for every good work"
(2 Corinthians 9:8).

TAKE OUT

"If you wish to dwell in the house of many mansions,
you must make your reservation in advance."

PRAYER *List*

_____

_____

_____

_____

_____

_____

_____

_____

_____

_____

_____

_____

_____

_____

_____

ENDNOTES

Chapter 1

1 The term "God is dead" is attributed to Friedrich Nietzche, who first coined it in his book *The Gay Science* (1882, 1887) section 125. His ideas about a new system of morality were further developed by Joseph Fletcher in his book *Situation Ethics: The New Morality* (Louisville: Westminster John Knox Press, 1966, 1998) For a further sketch of Nietzche's philosophy see www.en.wikipedia.org/wiki/Godisdead, 7 Jan. 2011.

2 Jill Jackson and Sy Miller, "Let There Be Peace on Earth." © 1955 by Jan-Lee Music. Copyright renewed 1983. International copyright secured. All rights reserved.

3 C.B. McAfee, "Near to the Heart of God" (1903).

Chapter 2

1 Julie Garden-Robinson, "Ingredient Substitutions," *ag.ndsu.edu*, North Dakota State University, July 1999. Web. 7 Jan. 2011.

2 Wayne Jackson, *The Human Body: Accident or Design?* (Stockton: Courier, 1993, 2000) 36.

3 Gregg Easterbrook, *The Progress Paradox: How Life Gets Better While People Feel Worse* (New York: Random House Trade Paperbacks, 2004) 163-164. Easterbrook lays out a comprehensive case for how life in America and Europe has improved since World War II, but he adds that the trend line for happiness has been flat for 50 years and negative for those who consider themselves "very happy." He

reports that 10 times as many people in Western nations suffer from "unipolar" depression today than did half a century ago. He writes, "Americans and Europeans have ever more of everything except happiness."

4 W.E. Vine, Merrill F. Unger and William White Jr., *Vine's Complete Expository Dictionary of Old and New Testament Words* (Nashville: Thomas Nelson, 1984, 1996) 284.

5 S.I. McMillen, *None of These Diseases* (Grand Rapids: Fleming H. Revell, 1963, 1993) preface. Revised edition © 2000 by David E. Stern.

Chapter 3
1 Sara (Dolly) Leighton, *Shine Like Stars* (Nashville: Gospel Advocate, 2005) 10.

Chapter 4
1 Shad Helmstetter, *What to Say When You Talk to Yourself* (New York: Simon & Schuster, 1982) 163.

2 W.E. Vine, *An Expository Dictionary of New Testament Words*, Vol. 1 (Old Tappan: Fleming Revell, 1940, 1966) 55.

3 Bill W. Flatt, *Since You Asked* (Abilene: Quality, 1983) 162-163.

4 Vine, *An Expository Dictionary*, Vol. 4, 114.

5 William Blake, "A Poison Tree," *Bartlett's Familiar Quotations*, 16th ed., gen. eds. John Bartlett, Justin Kaplan (Boston: Little, Brown and Co., 1992) 358.

Chapter 5
1 Robert Boyd, *Boyd's Bible Handbook* (Iowa Falls: World Bible, 1991) 568.

2 Elton Trueblood, *The Humor of Christ* (San Francisco: Harper and Row, 1964, 1974) 23.

3 C.F. Keil and Franz Delitzsch, *Commentary on the Old Testament, Vol. 6: Proverbs, Ecclesiastes, Song of Solomon* (Grand Rapids: Eerdmans, 1966, 1973, 1982, 1986, 2006) 233.

4 Trueblood 23.

5 McMillen 64-65.

Chapter 6

1 Joseph Swain, "How Sweet, How Heavenly Is the Sight," Walworth Hymns (1792).

2 Matthew Arnold, *The Works of Matthew Arnold in Fifteen Volumes*, Vol. 9 (London: Macmillan & Co. Ltd., Smith Elder & Co., 1904) 285. Qtd. in Vine.

3 Vine, Vol. 2, 117 ("forbearance"), 144-145 ("gentleness").

4 Edwin Markham, *The Shoes of Happiness and Other Poems* (New York: Doubleday, 1915). From the poem "Outwitted."

5 Thomas Carlyle, *Latter-Day Pamphlets*, 1850. Attributed originally to Napoleon by James Rogers, *The Dictionary of Clichés* (New York: Facts on File Publications, 1985) <http://www.phrases.org.uk/bulletinboard/37/messages/594.html> (accessed 1/07/11).

Chapter 8

1 "Foodborne Illness." Centers for Disease Control and Prevention. Dec. 23, 2010. U.S. Department of Health and Human Services. Jan. 5, 2011 <www.cdc.gov/ncidod/dbmd/diseaseinfo/foodborneinfections_g.htm>.

2 Ralph Waldo Emerson, from the essay "Intellect" (1841).

3 Vine, Vol. 2, 173. Elsewhere translated as "grave."

4 "Television & Health" Compiled by TV_Free America, 1322 18th Street, NW, Washington, DC 20036 and quoting from the A.C. Nielsen Co. http://www.csun.edu/science/health/docs/tv&health.html (01/08/11) (no author listed)

5 "Facts and TV Statistics," Parents Television Council http://www.parentstv.org/ptc/facts/mediafacts.asp (01/08/11) (no author listed)

6 The topic of sexual addiction in women and its link to pornography is explored at length by Marnie C. Ferree, a licensed marriage and family therapist and the author of *No Stones* (Fairfax: Xulon, 2002).

7 Norman Vincent Peale, *The Power of Positive Thinking* (New York: Ballantine Books, 1952, 1956) 23.

8 W.H. Channing, as quoted by Arthur Brisbane, "William Henry Channing's Symphony." Editorial, Hearst Newspapers, c. 1920.

Chapter 9

1 James I. Packer, Merrill C. Tenney, and William White, Jr., Editors, *The Bible Almanac* (Nashville: Thomas Nelson, 1980) 471.

Chapter 11

1 U.S. Department of Health and Human Services and U.S. Department of Agriculture, *Dietary Guidelines for Americans 2005* (Washington, DC: U.S. Government Printing Office, 2005). Other leading health authorities, including the National Academy of Sciences, the National High Blood Pressure Education Program, and the American Heart Association, recommend that Americans limit sodium intake to no more than 2,300 milligrams per day. <http://www.foodreference.com>.

2 <www.saltinstitute.org/uses-benefits>.

3 James A. Patch, "Salt," *International Standard Bible Encyclopedia*, Vol. 4, 1978 ed., 2664.

4 Patch 2664.

5 James Dobson, *The New Hide or Seek: Building Confidence in Your Child* (Grand Rapids: Revell, 1999) 203-223.

Chapter 12

1 Arnold 285.

2 Charles Davis Tillman and A.C. Palmer, "Ready to Suffer" (1903).

Recipe Index